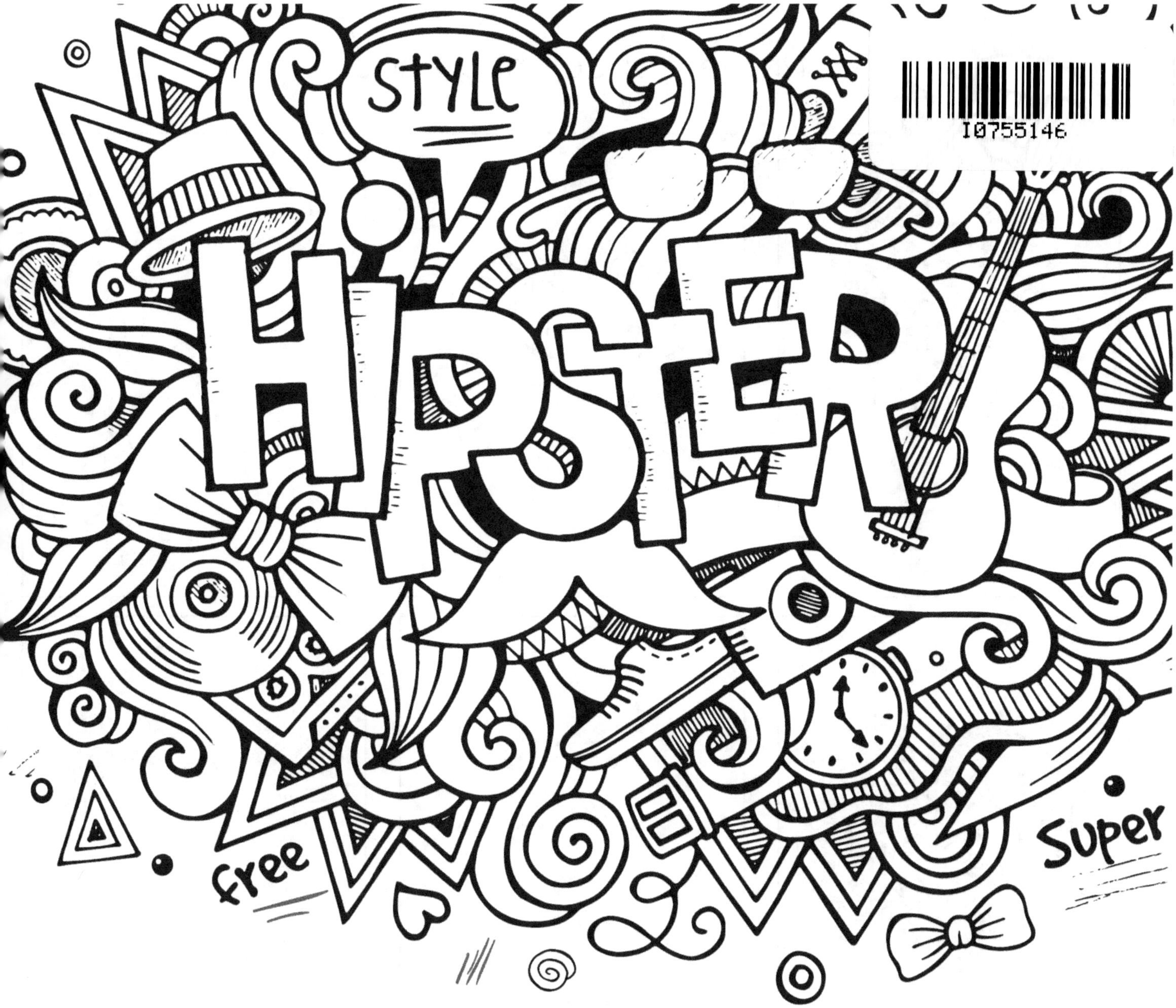

Coloring Book For Teens

Anti-Stress Designs Vol 3

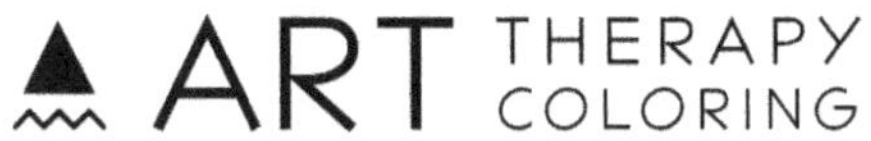

Preview of Coloring Pages

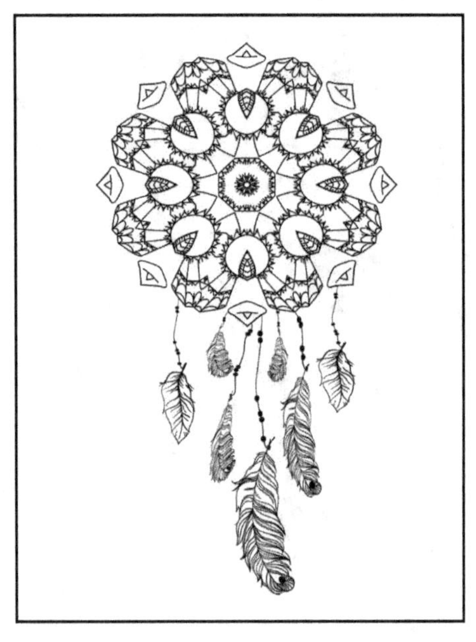

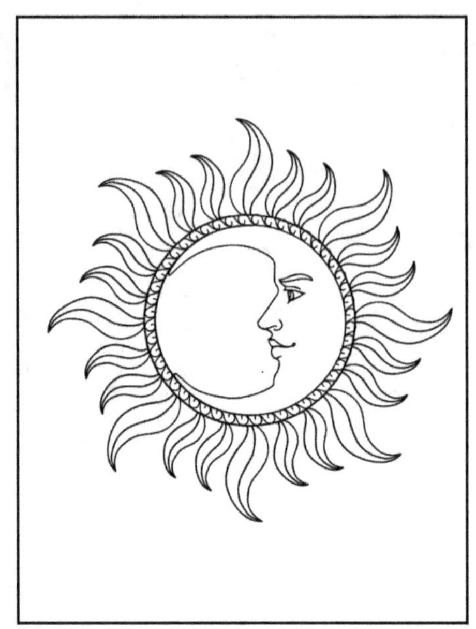

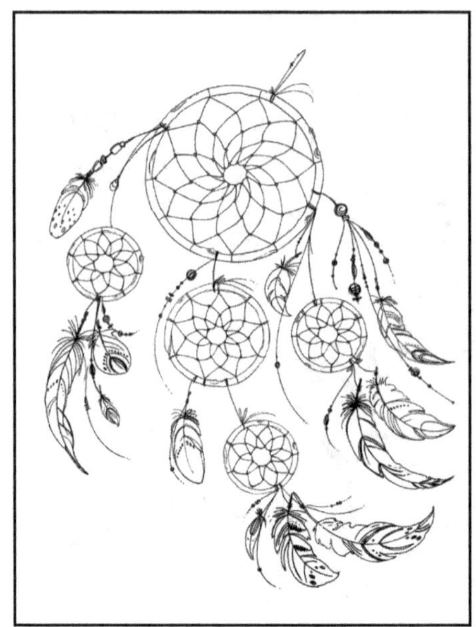

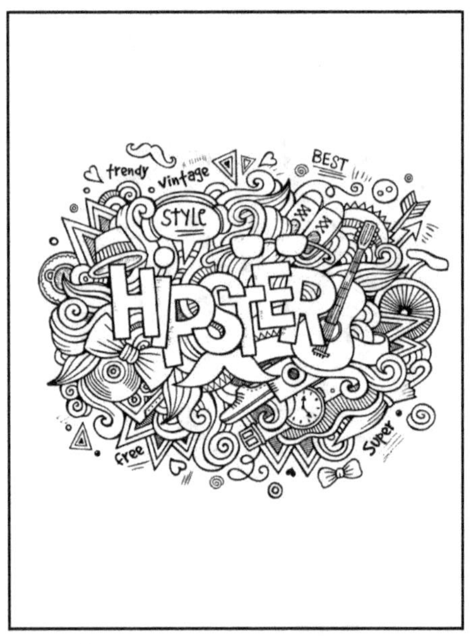

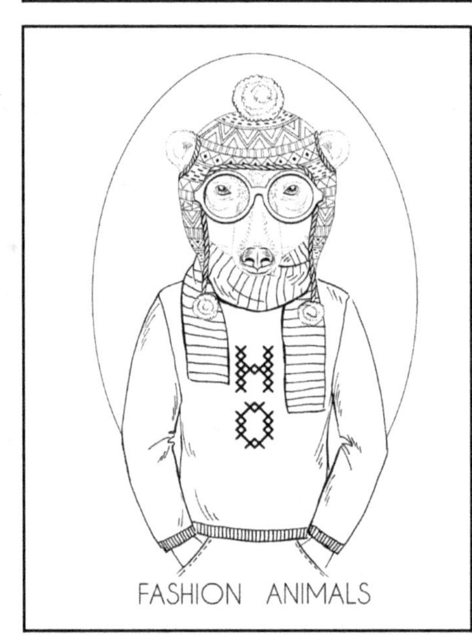

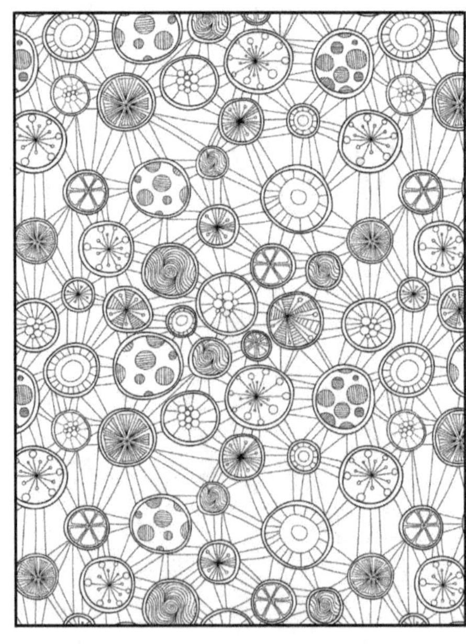

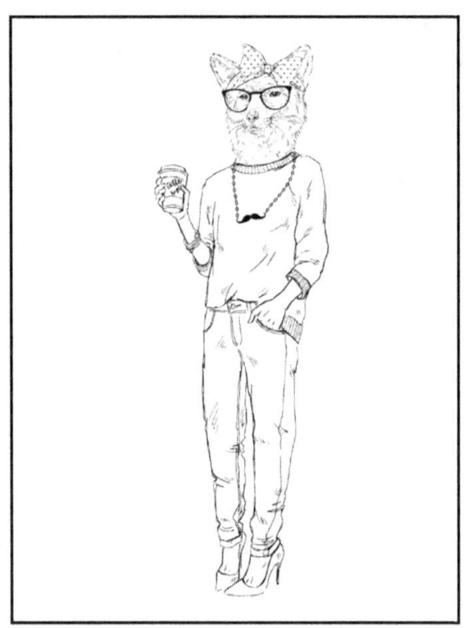

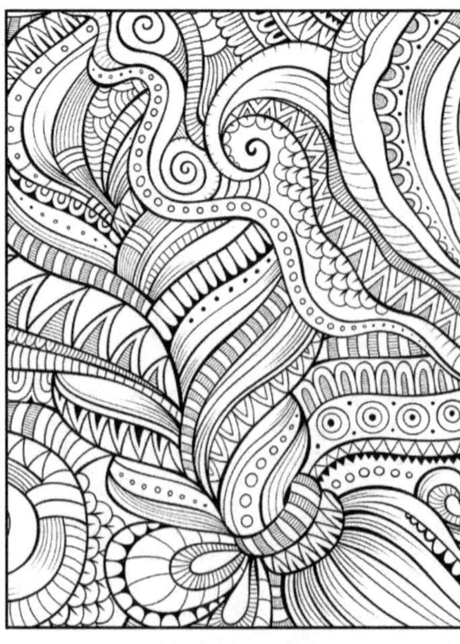

www.arttherapycoloring.com

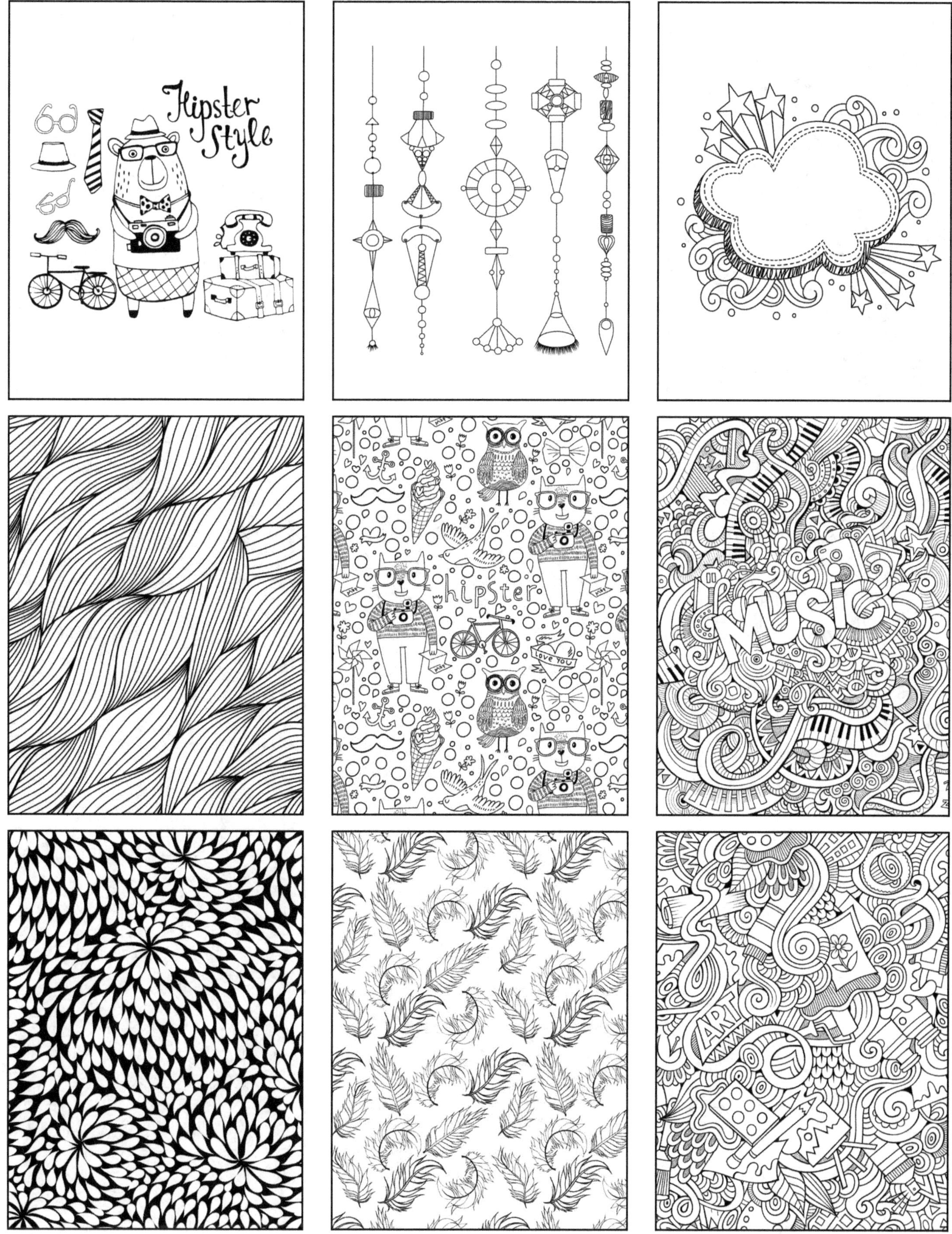

Preview of Coloring Pages

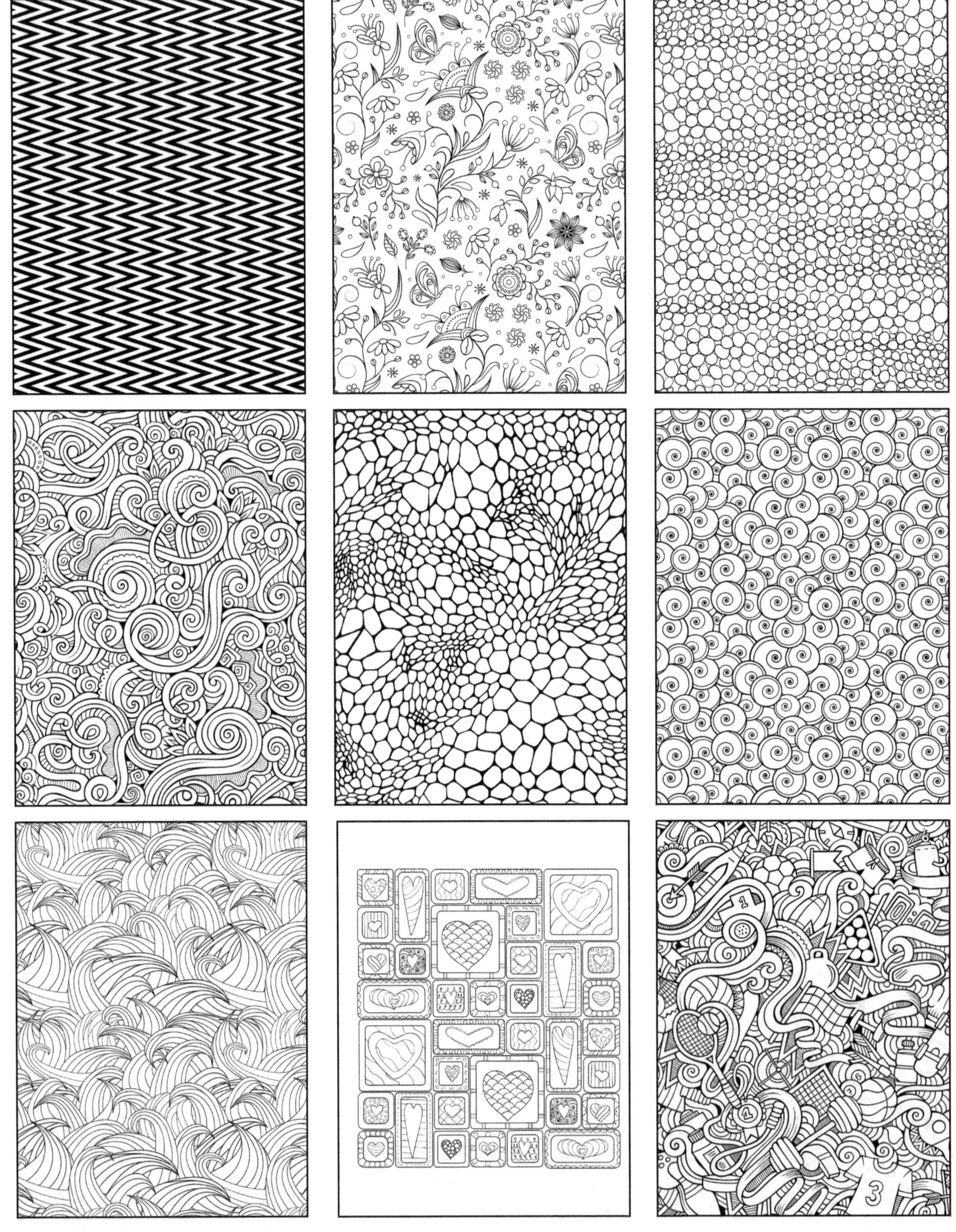

www.arttherapycoloring.com

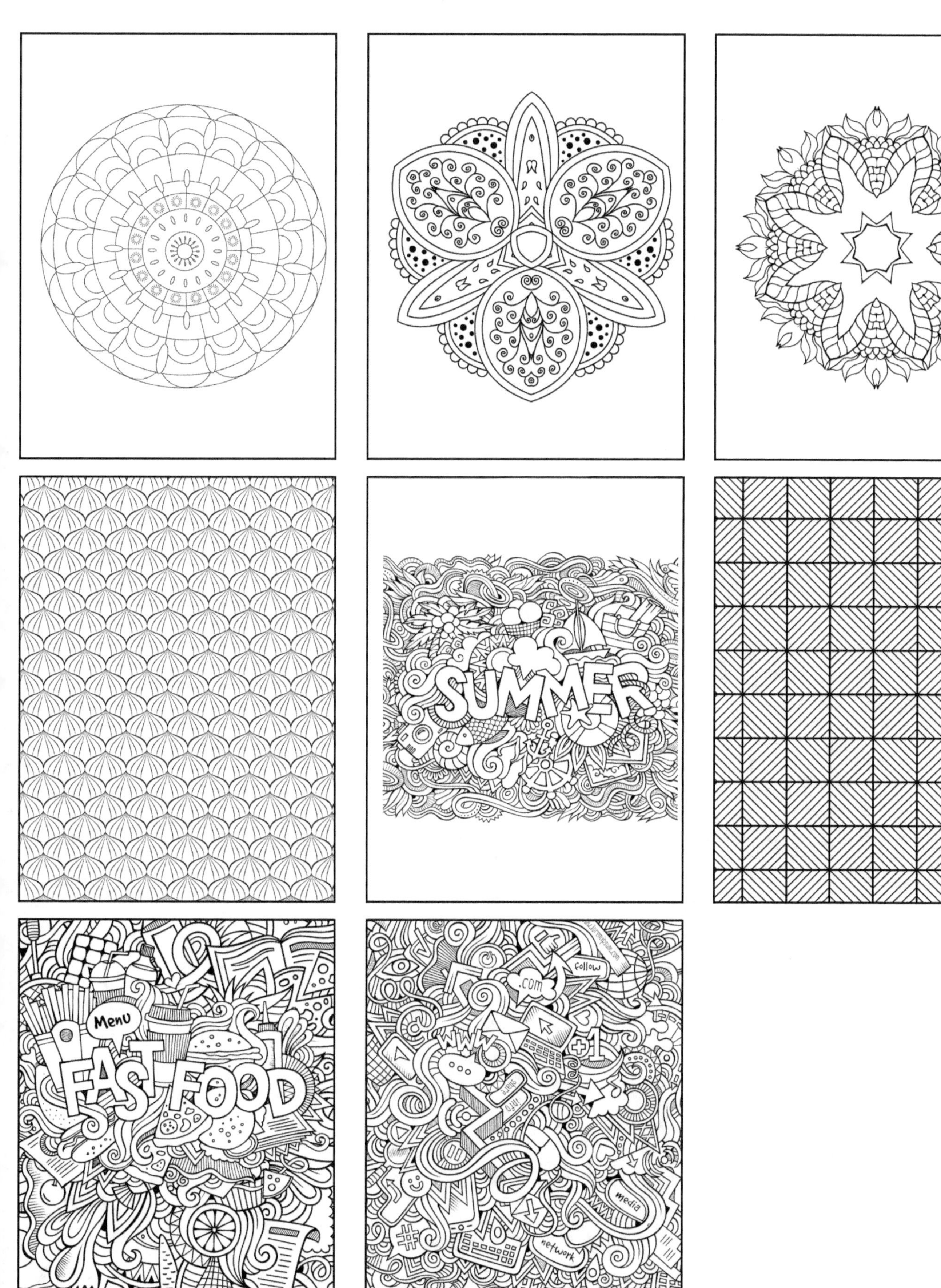

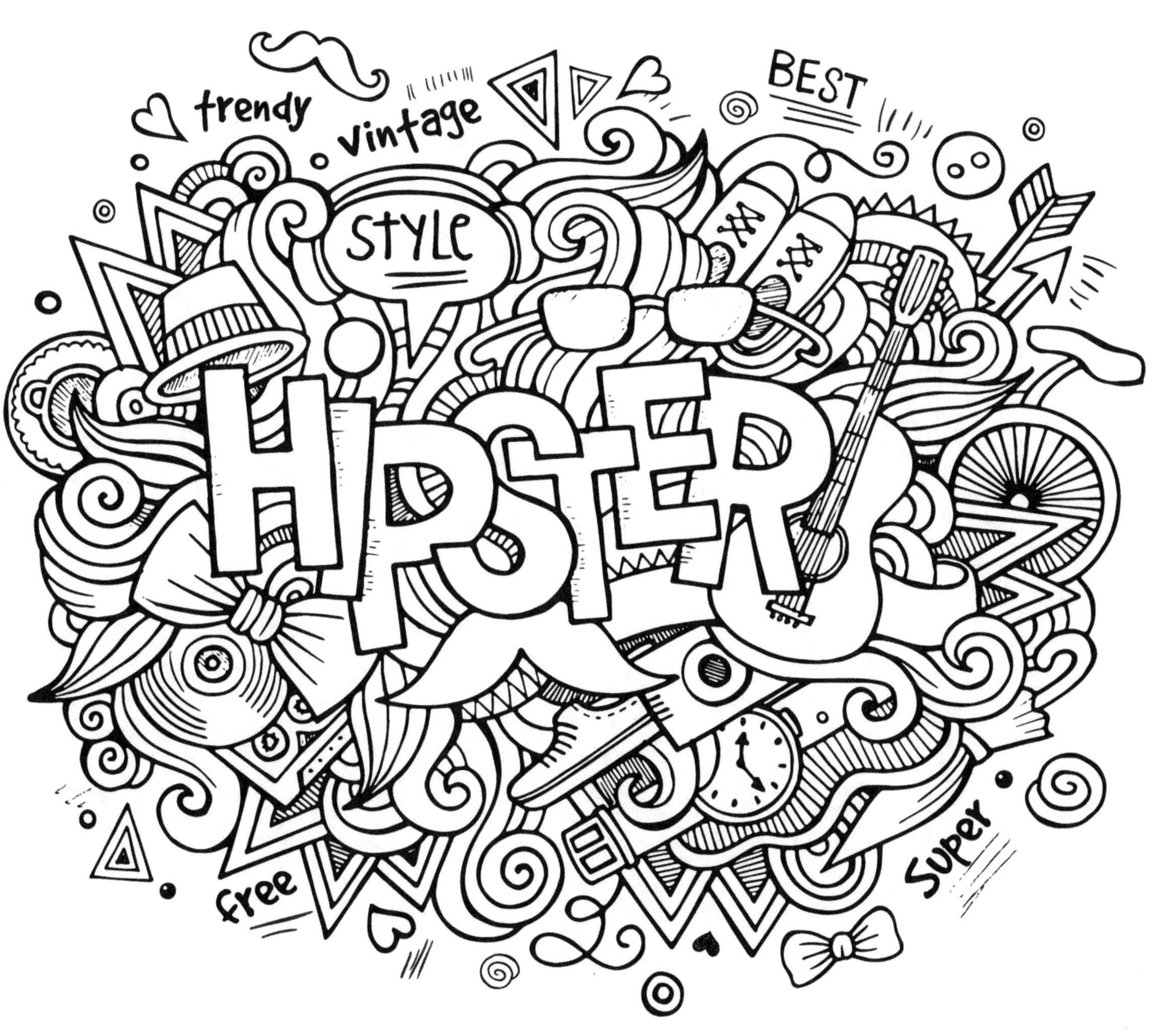
trendy
vintage
BEST
STYLE
HIPSTER
free
super

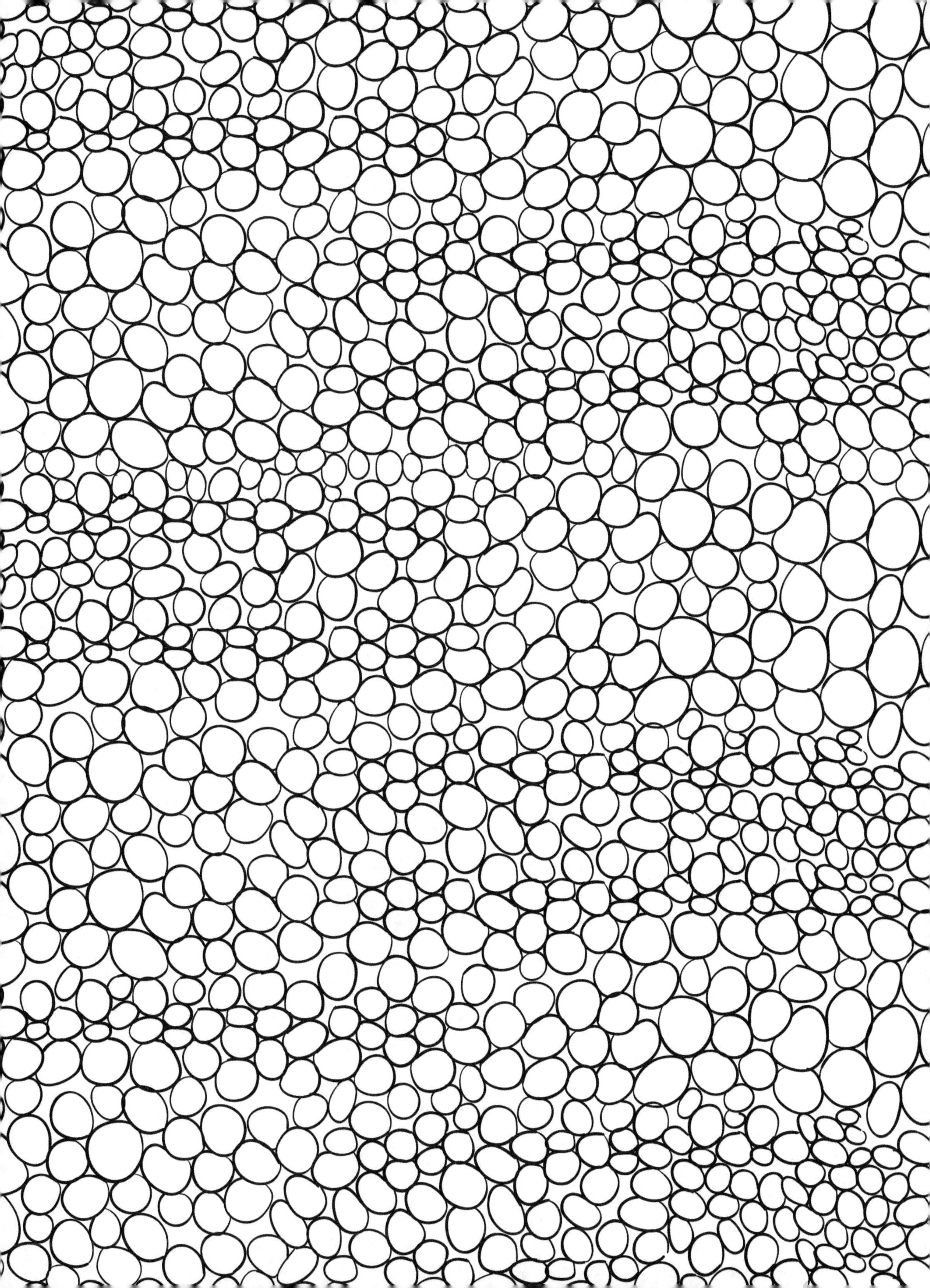

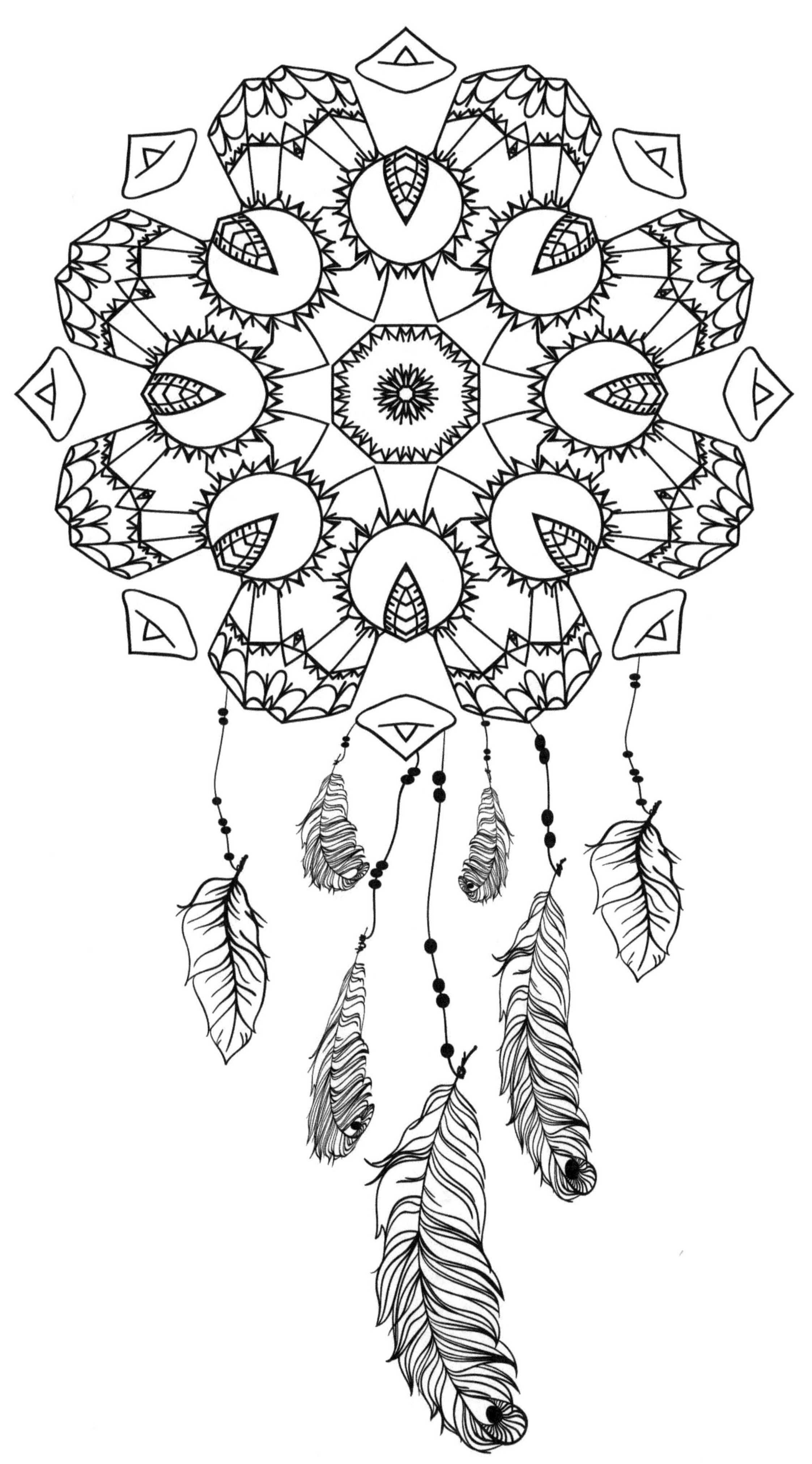

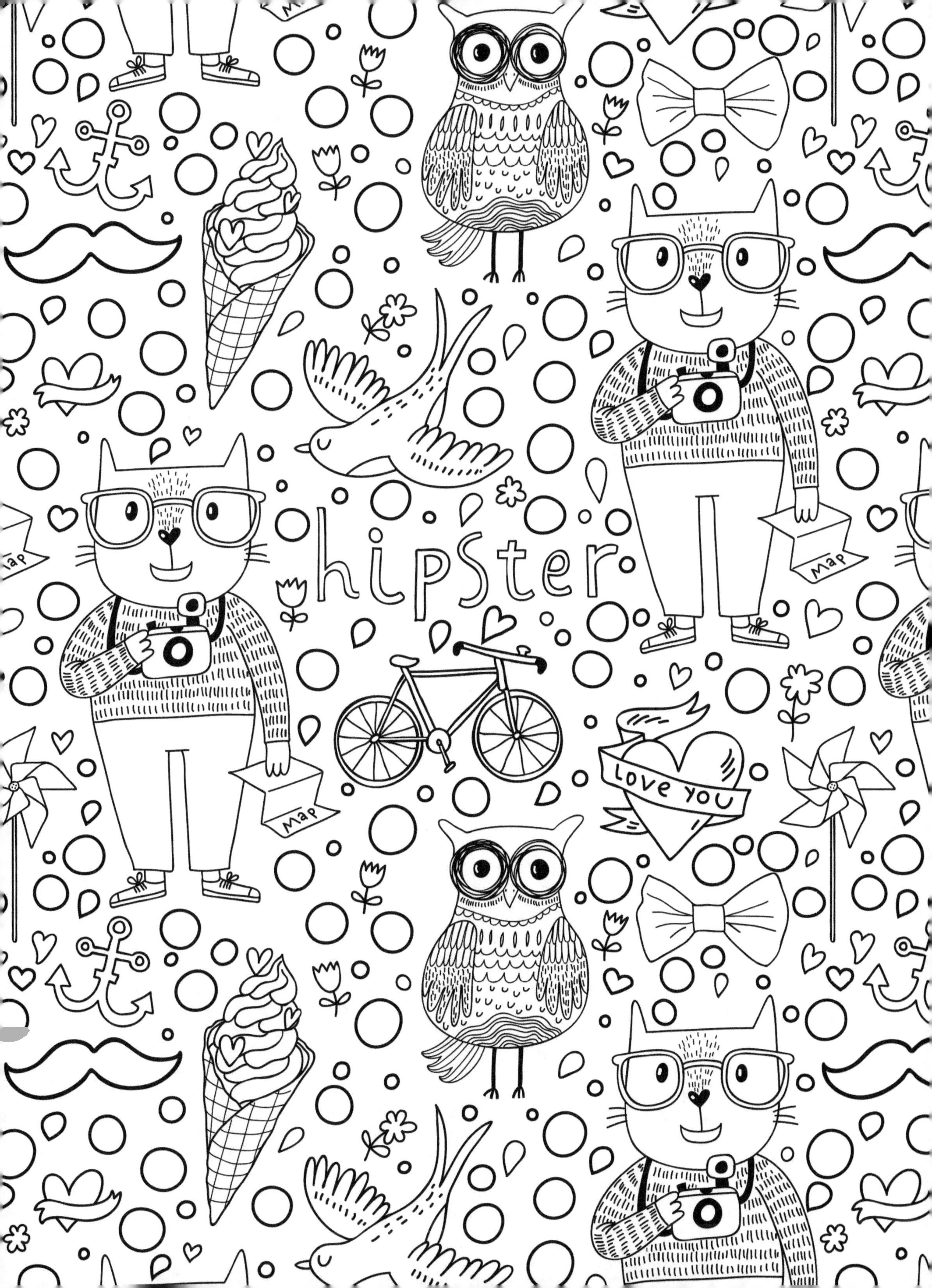
hipSter
Map
Map
Map
Love you

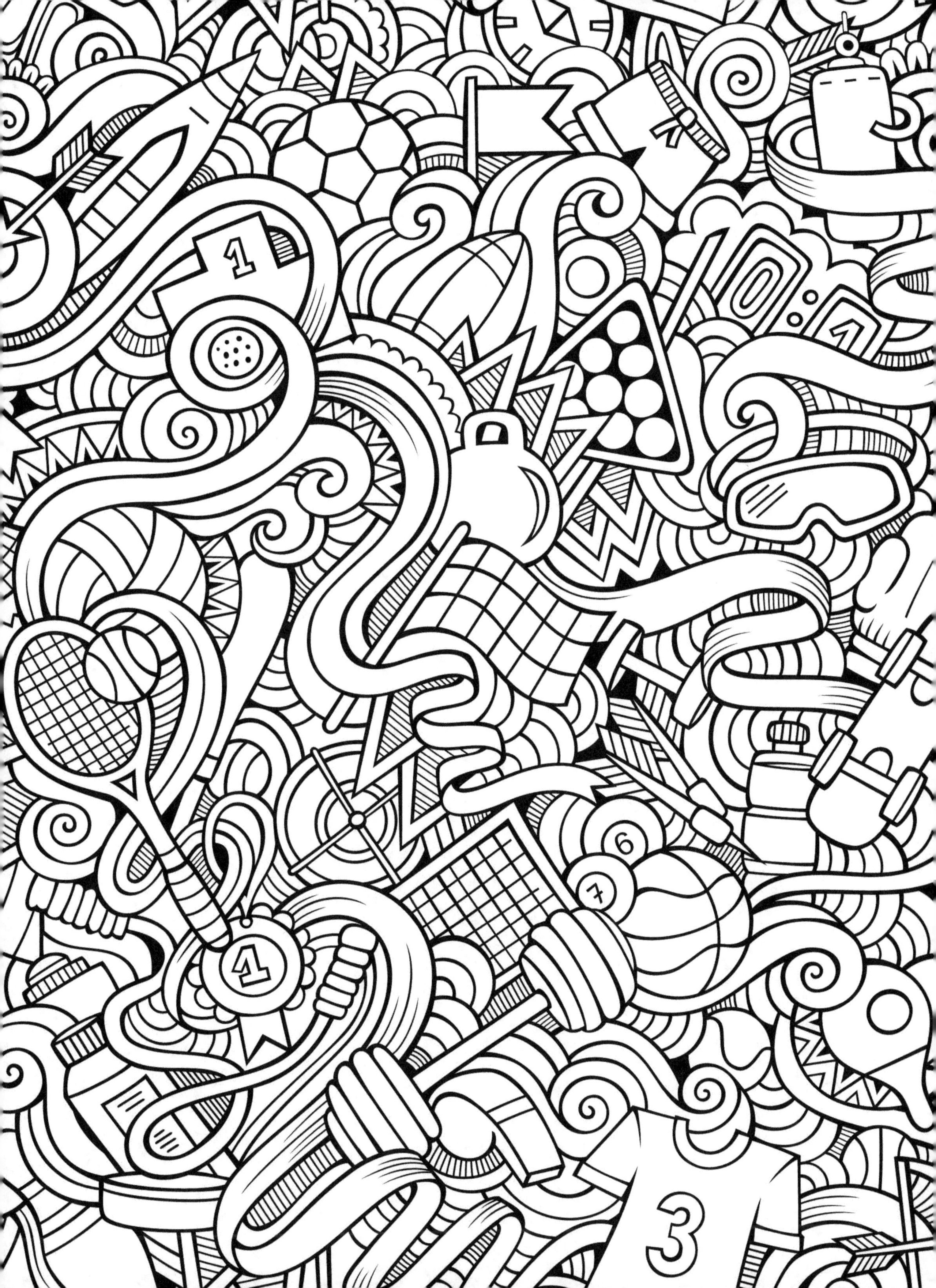
1
6
7
1
3

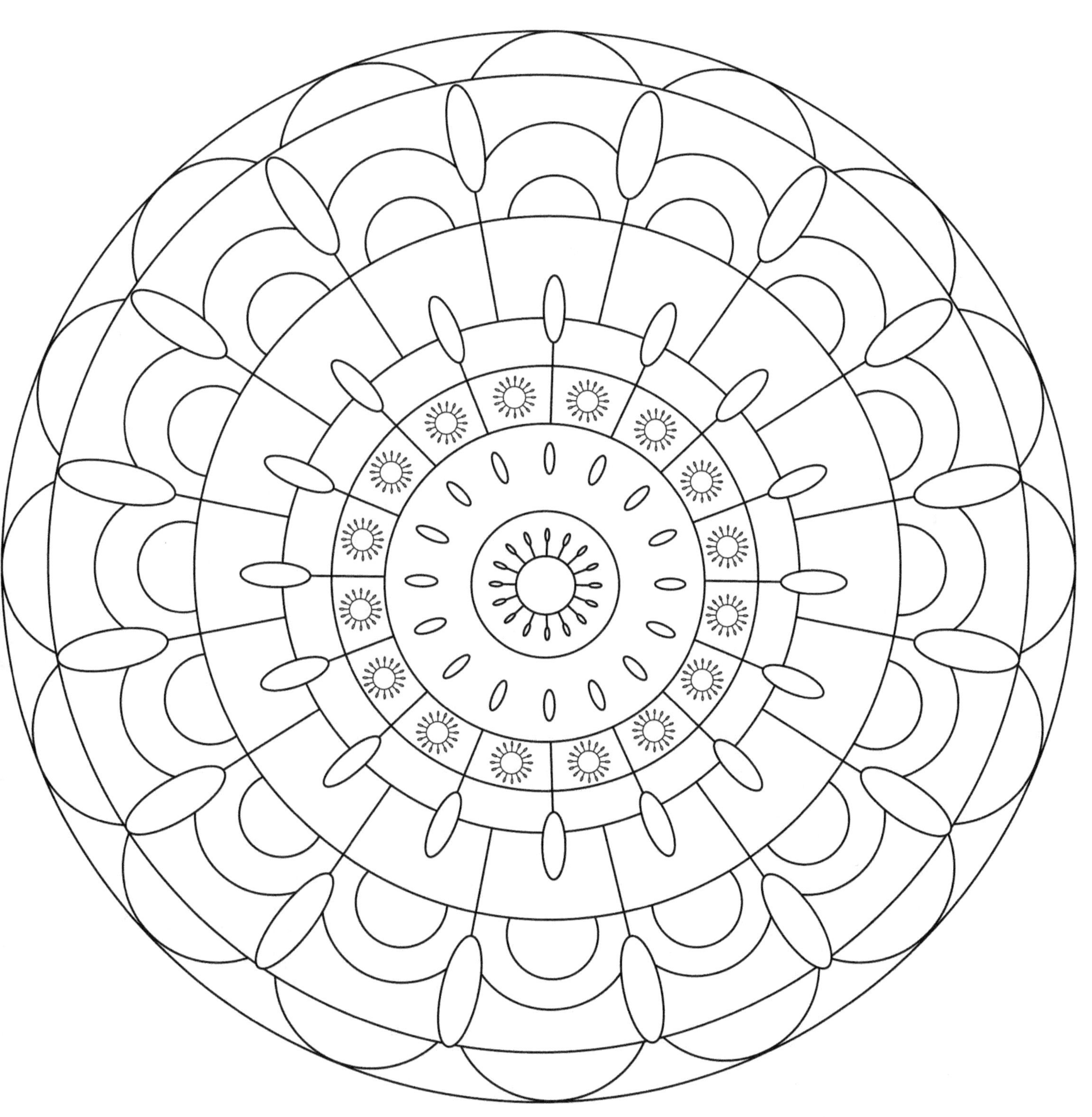

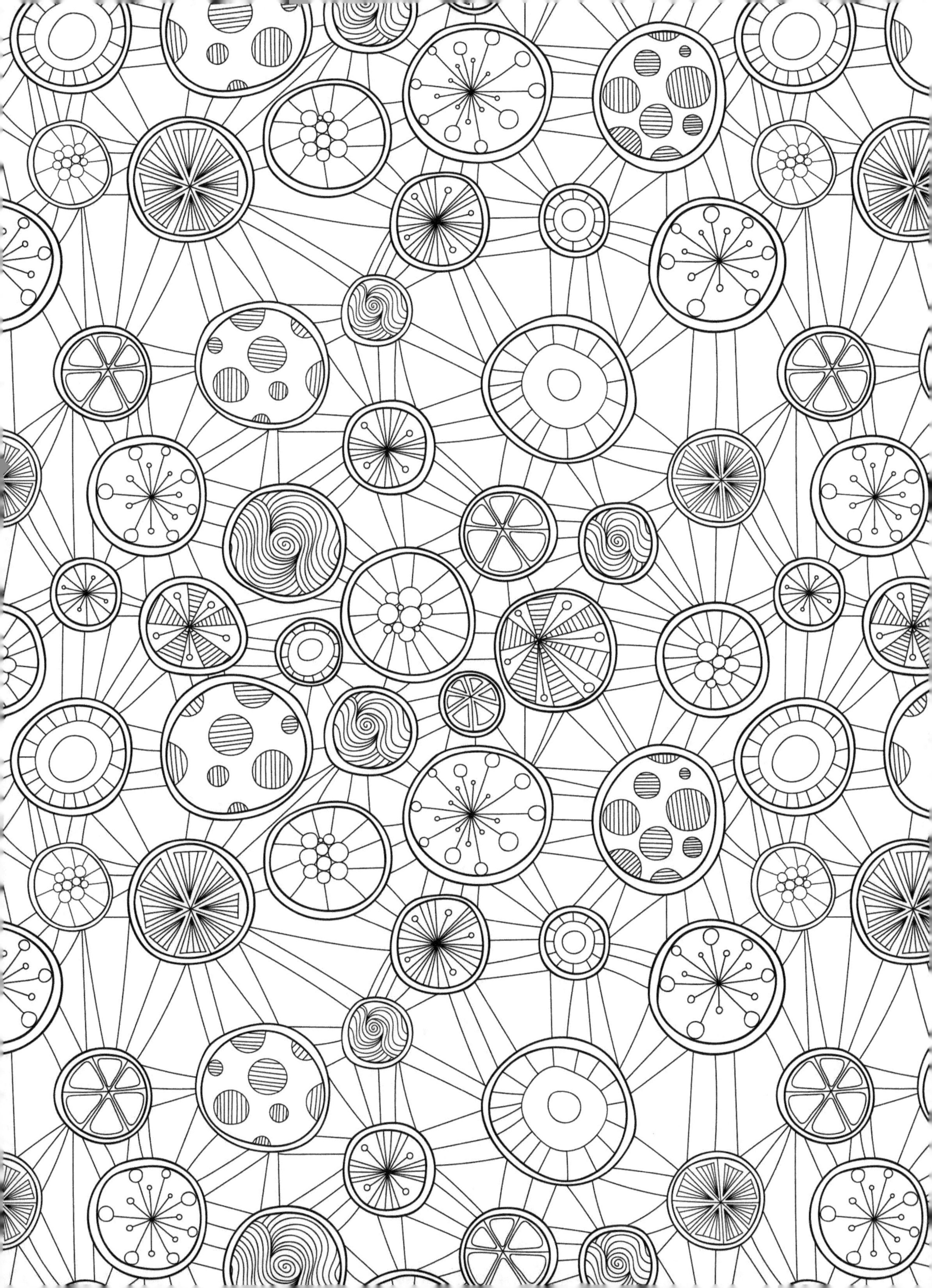

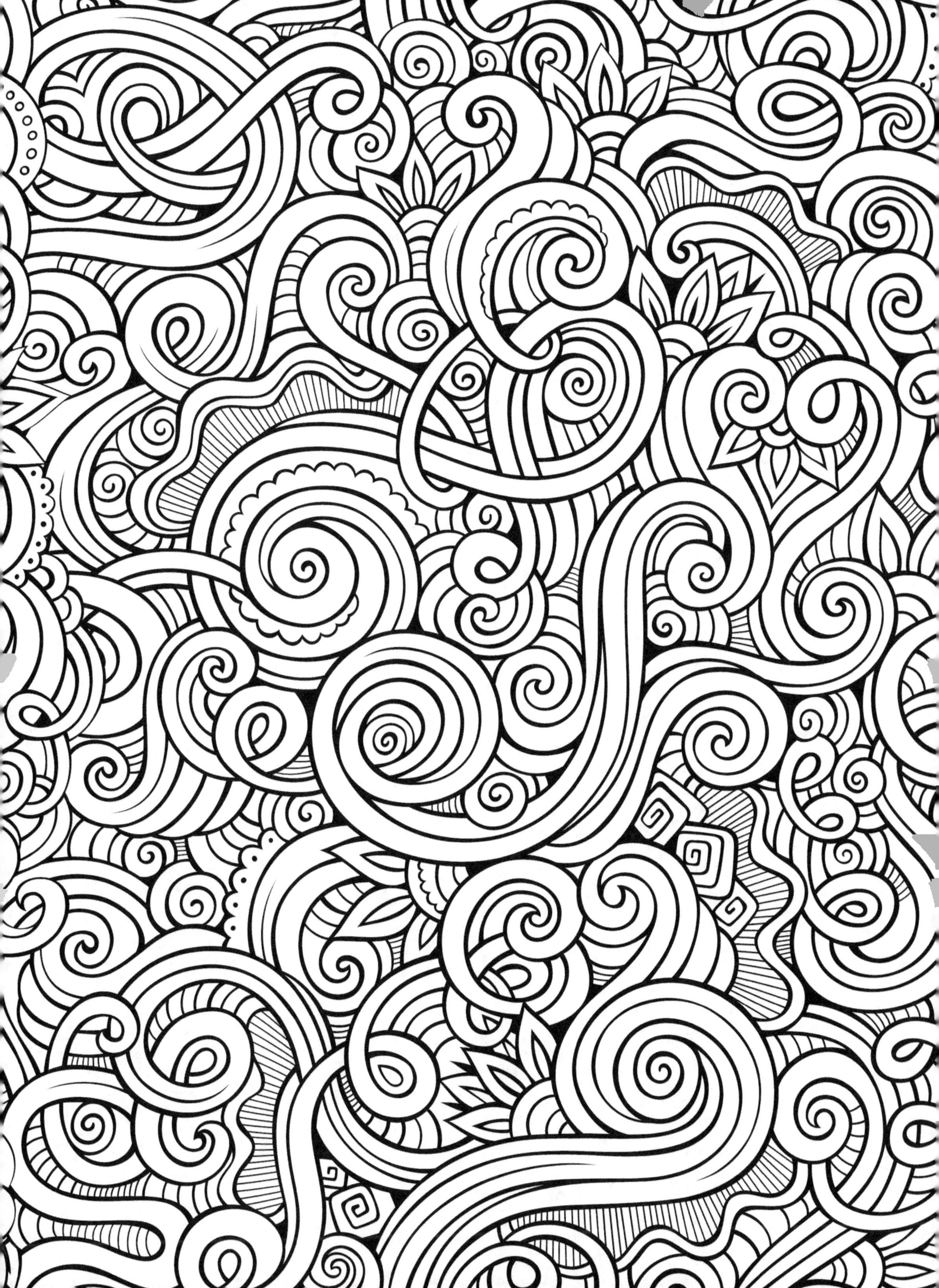

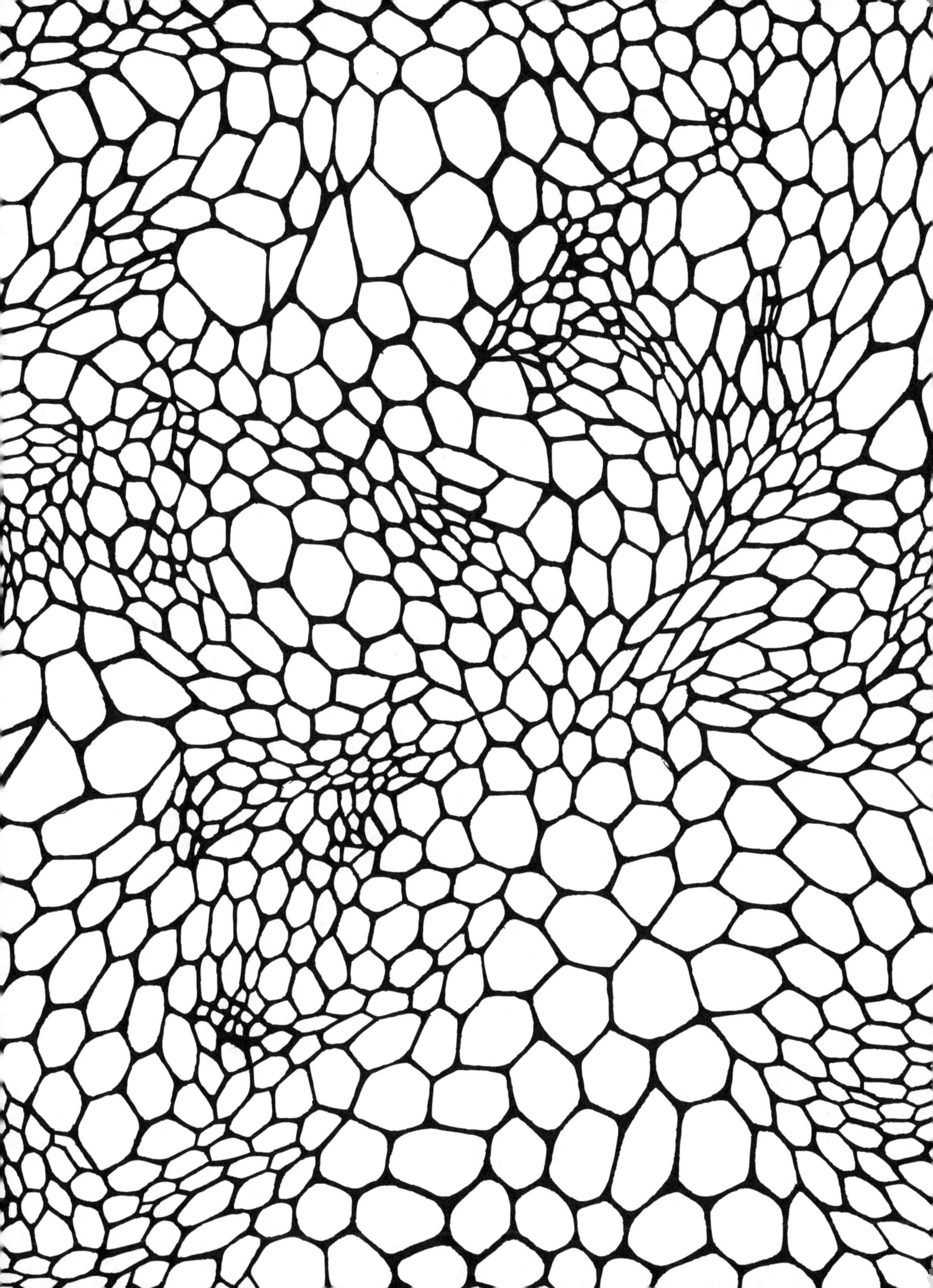

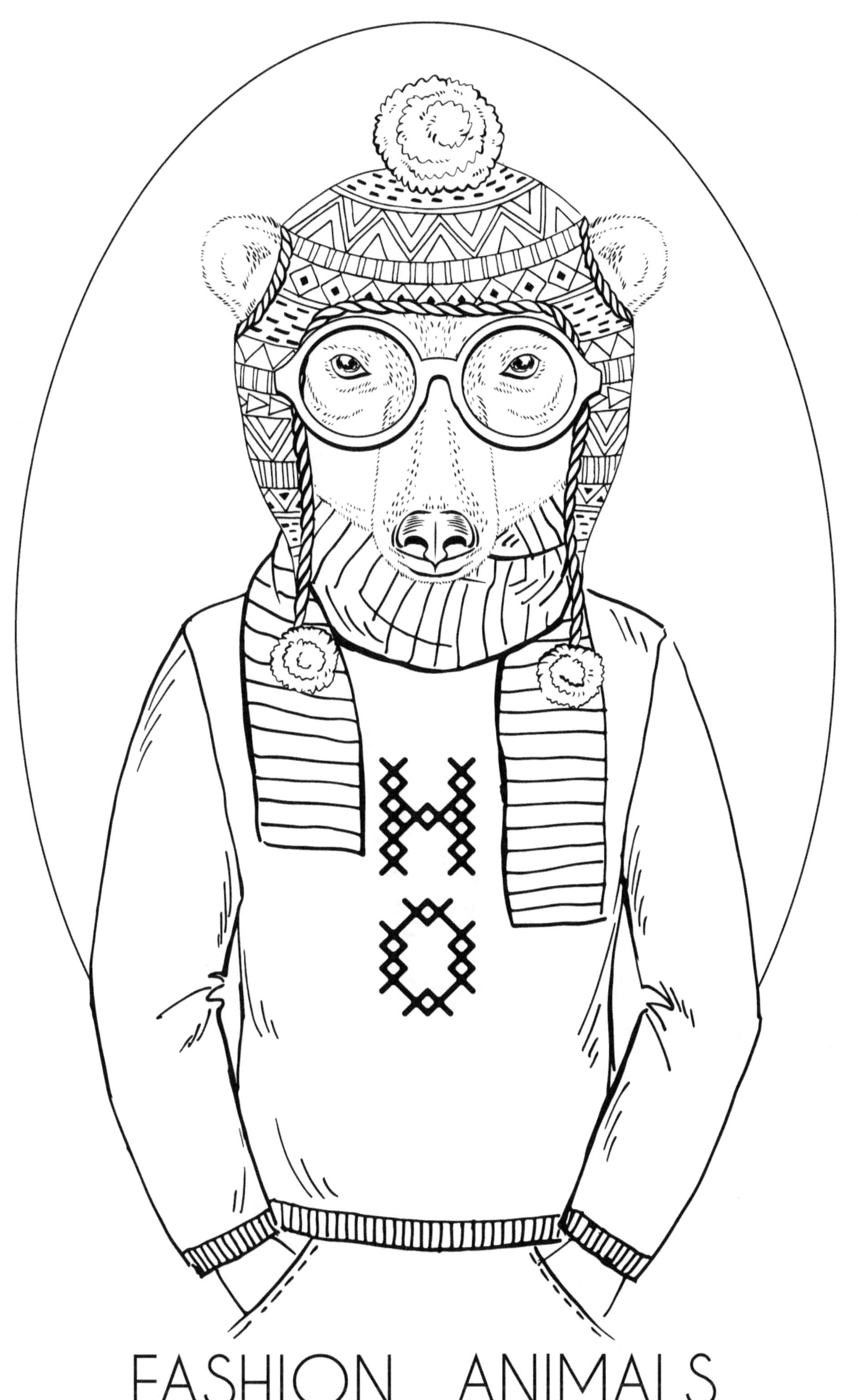

FASHION ANIMALS

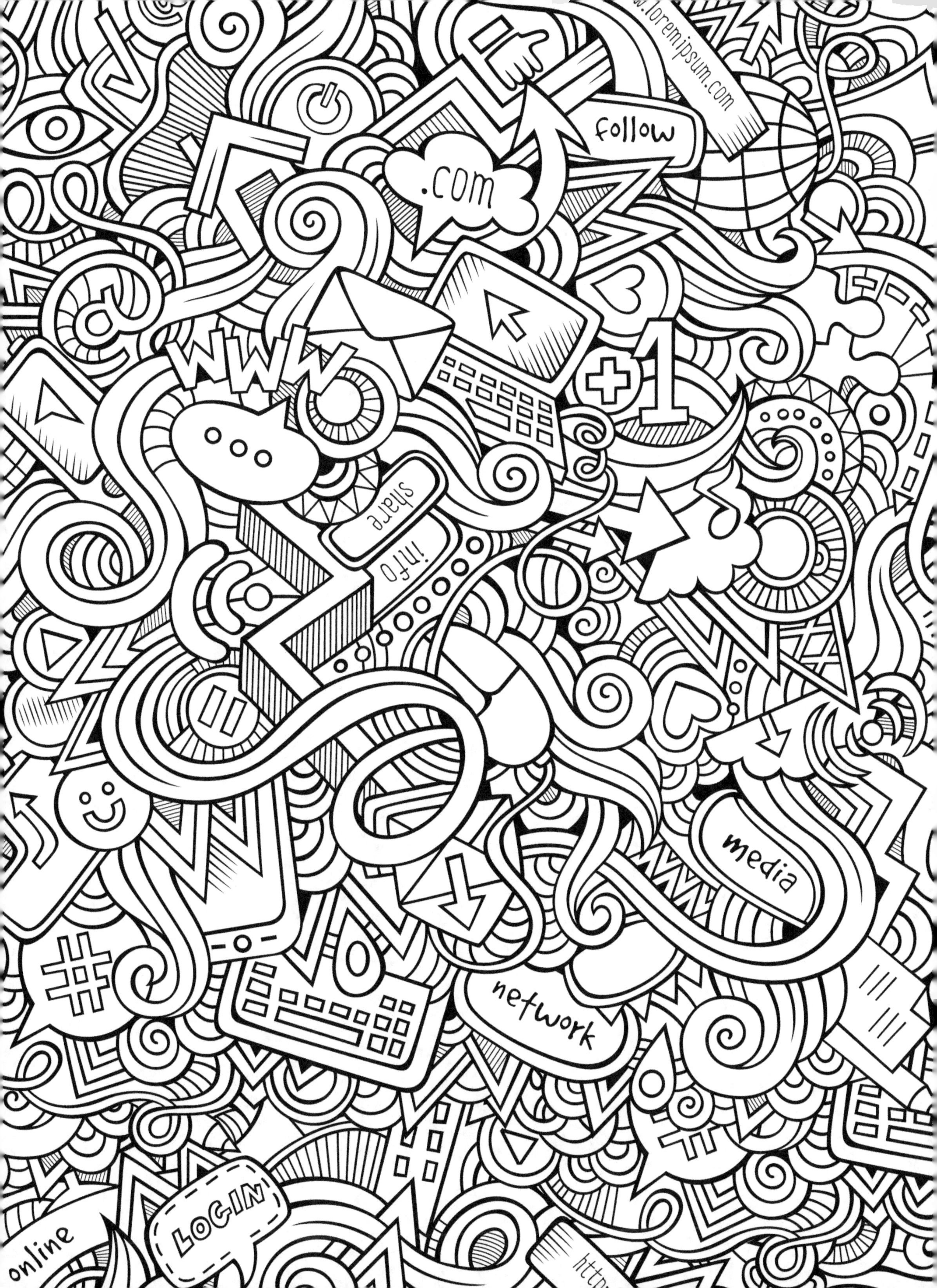
w.loremipsum.com
follow
.com
www
+1
share
info
media
network
LOGIN
online

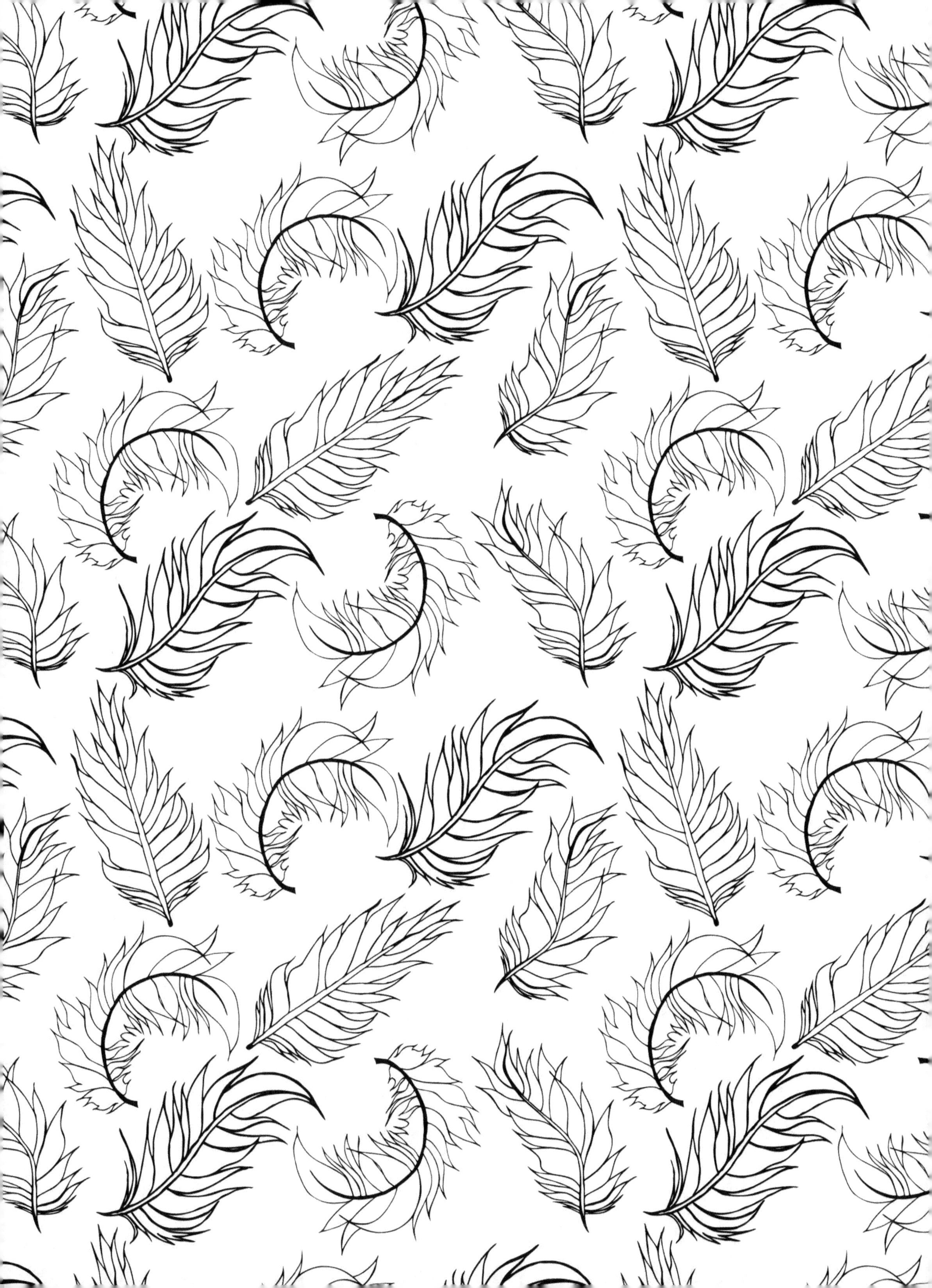

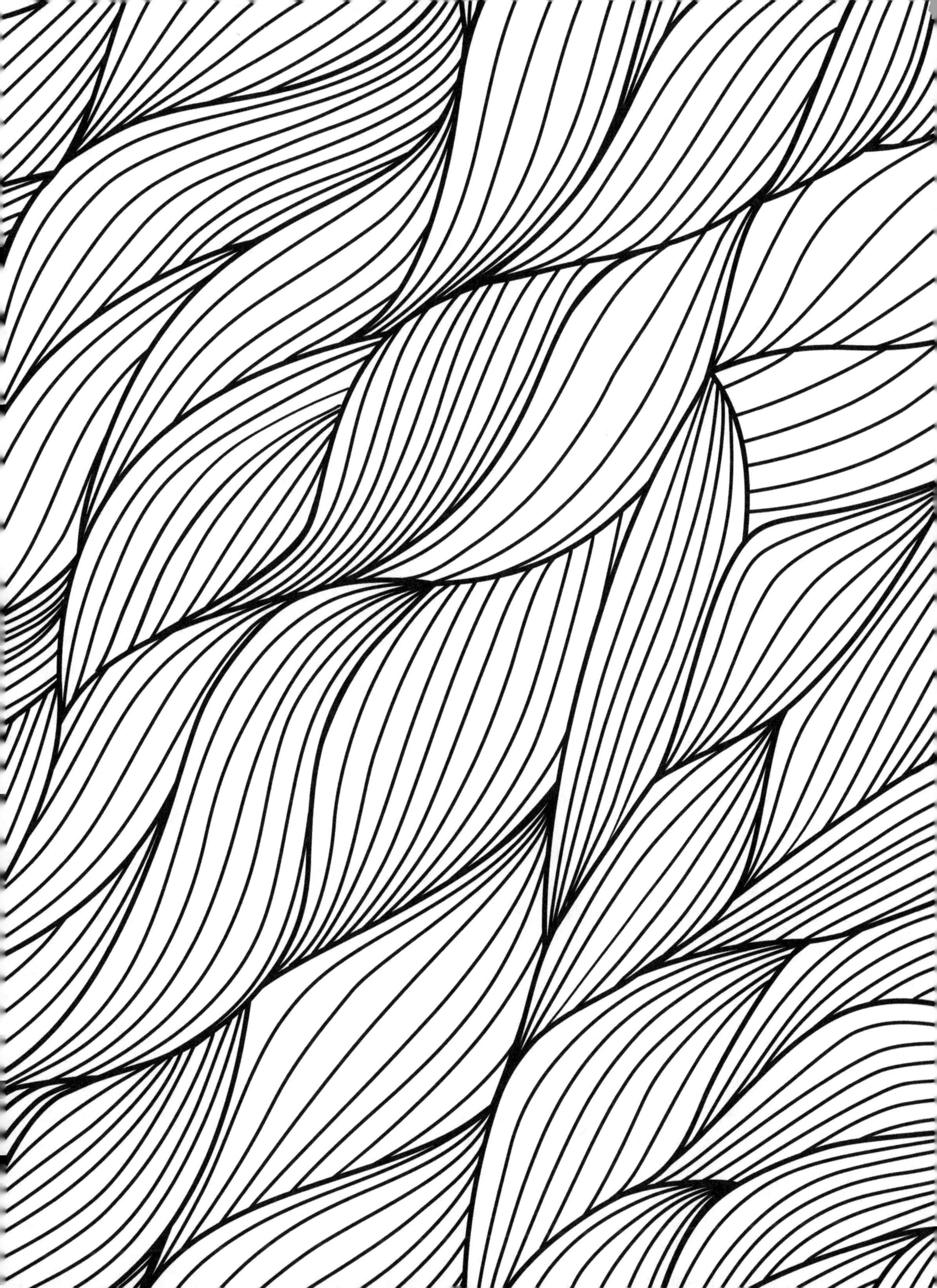

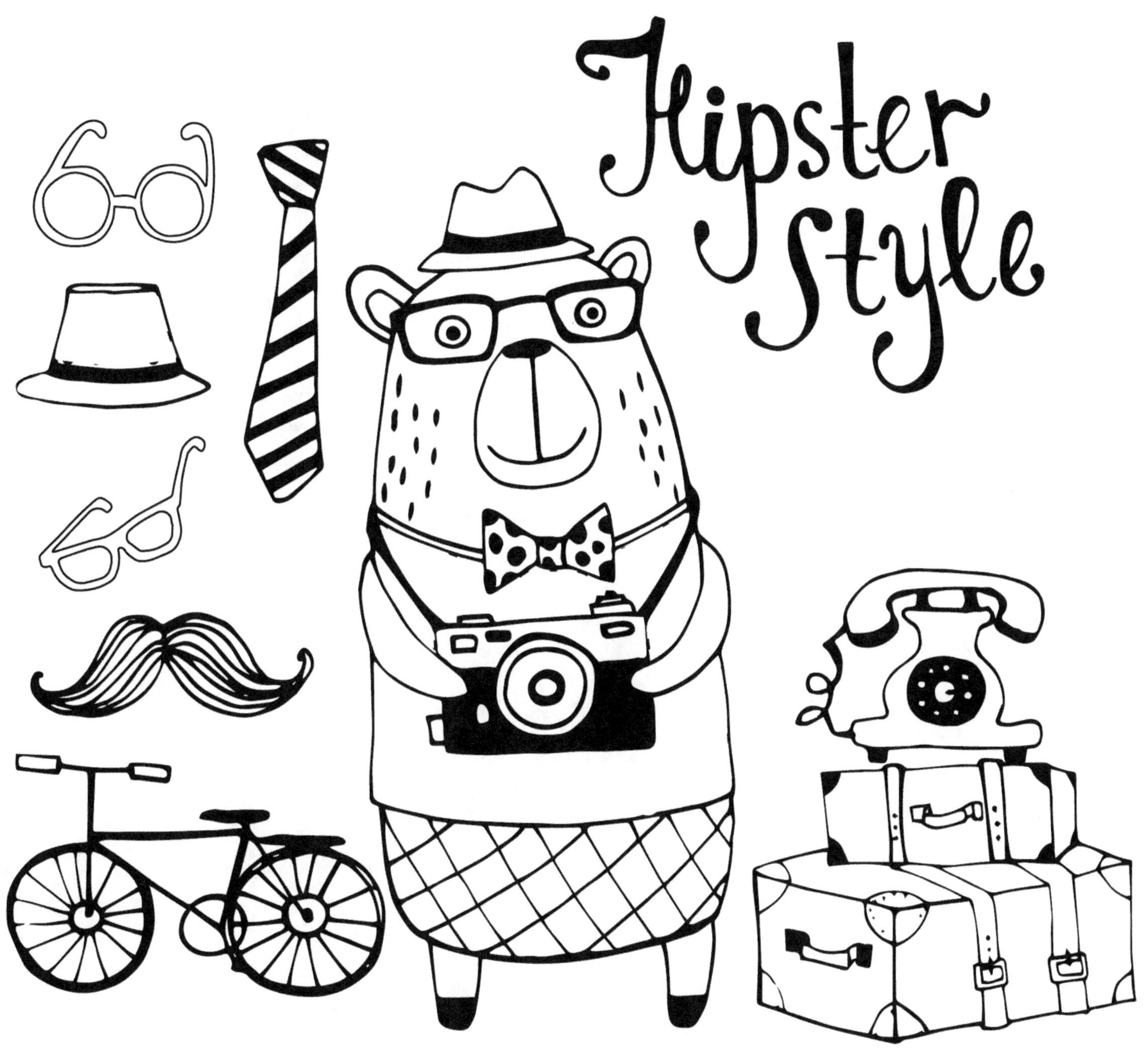
Hipster
Style

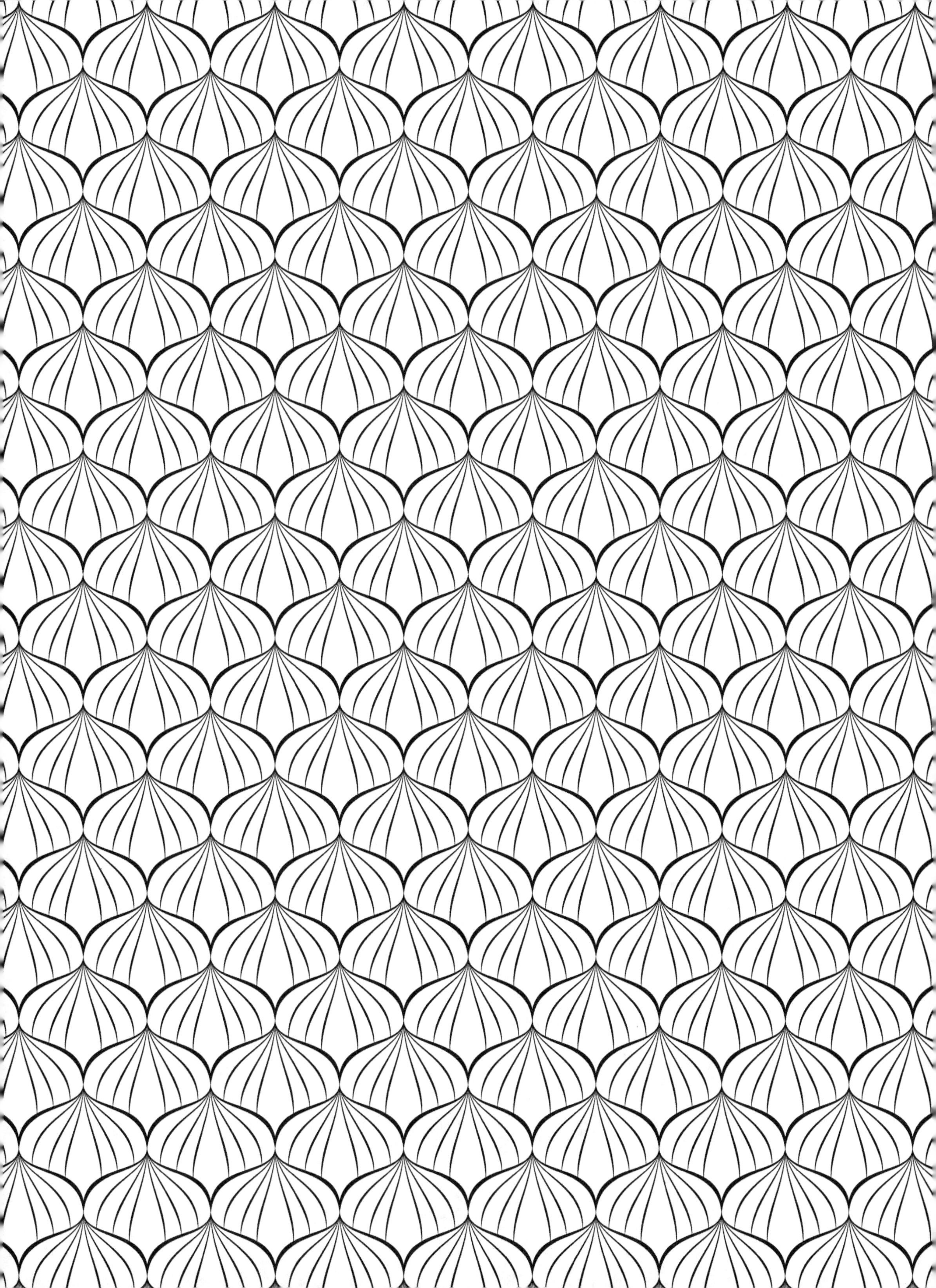

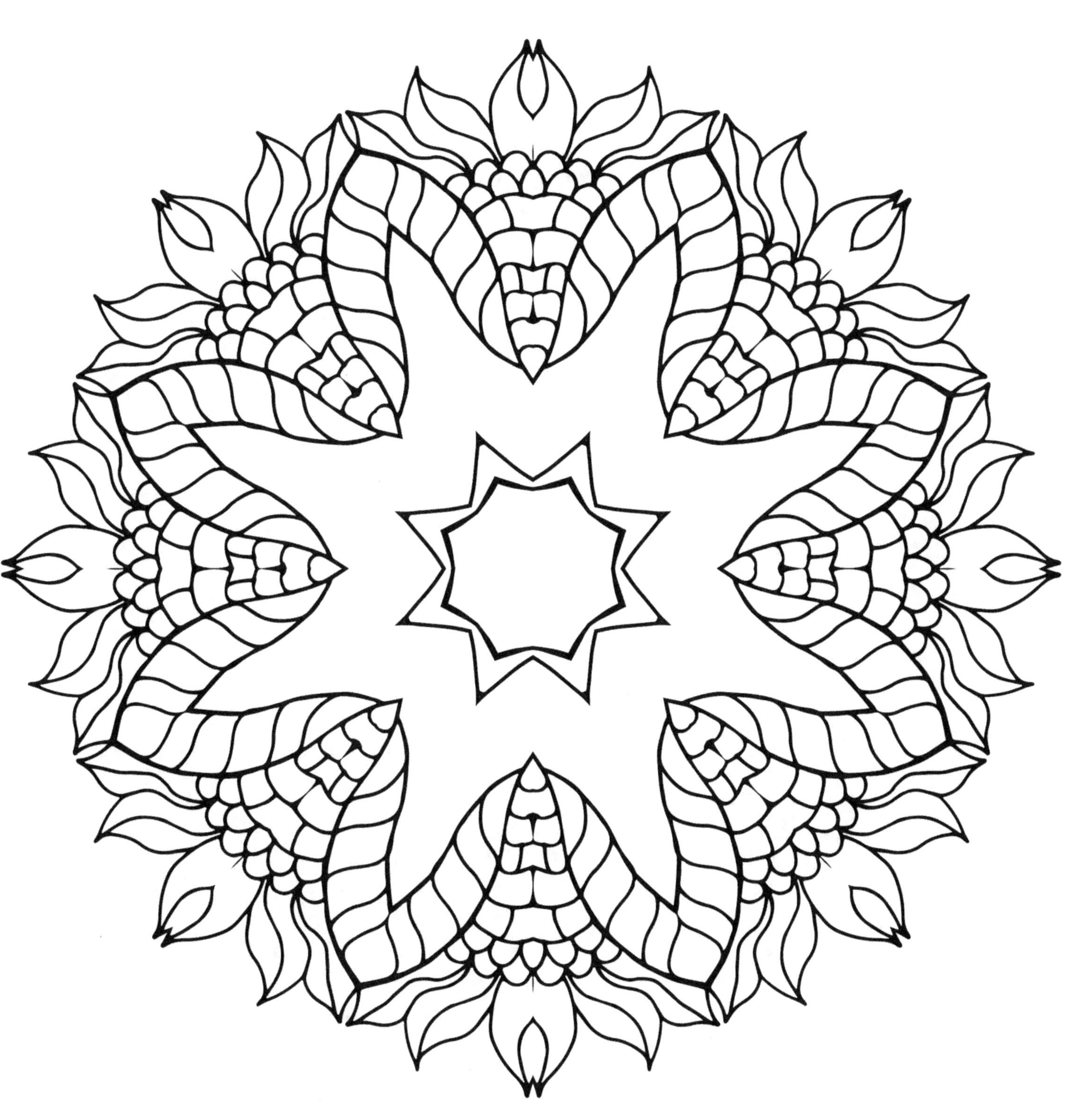

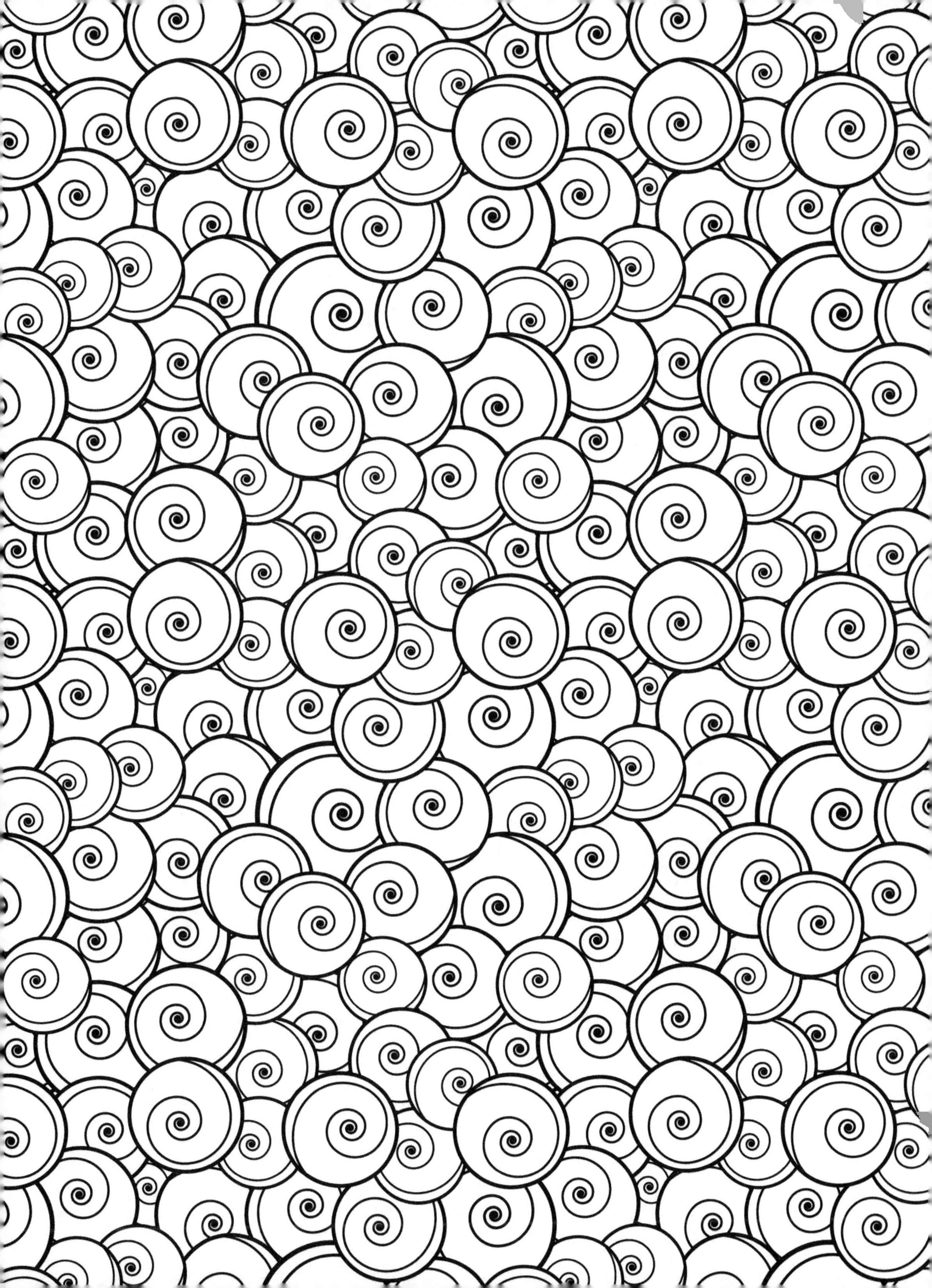

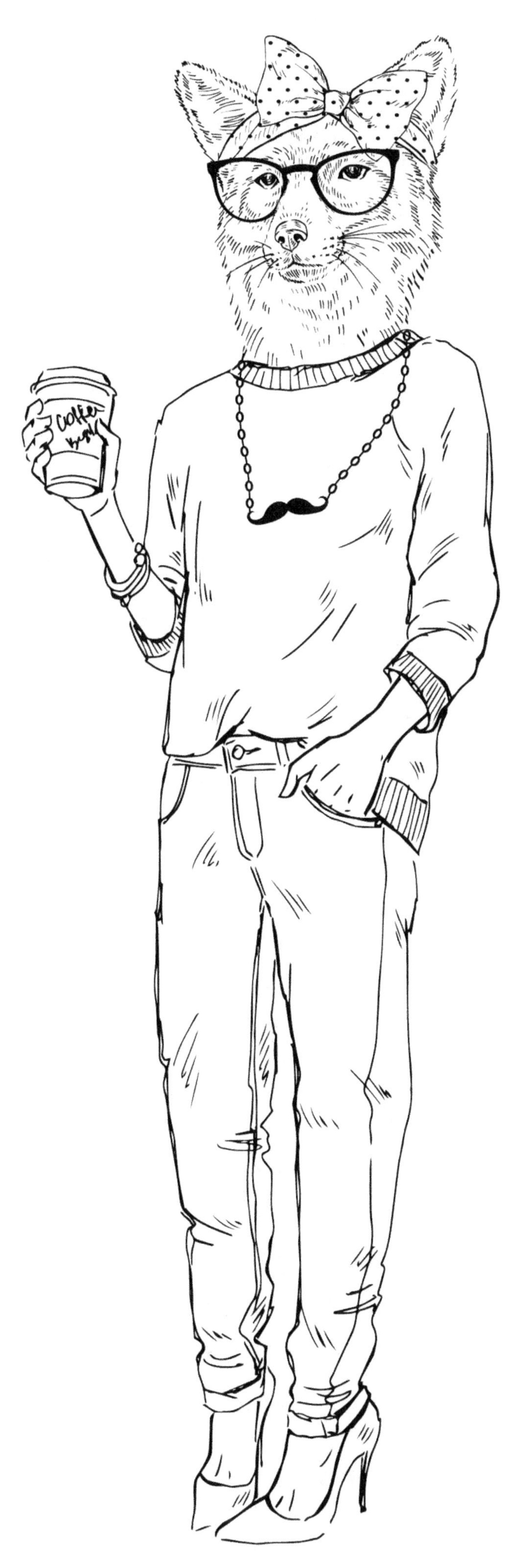

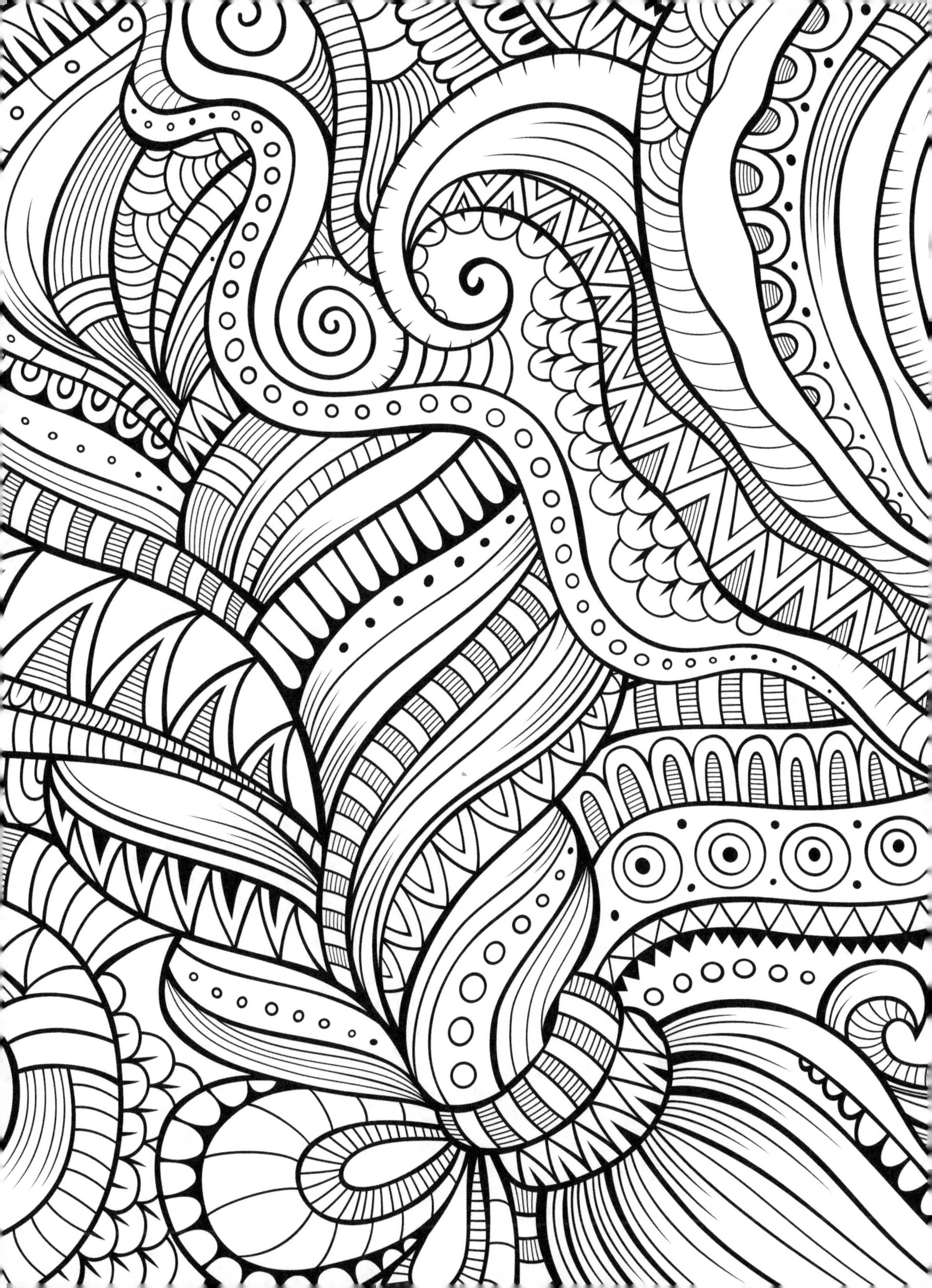

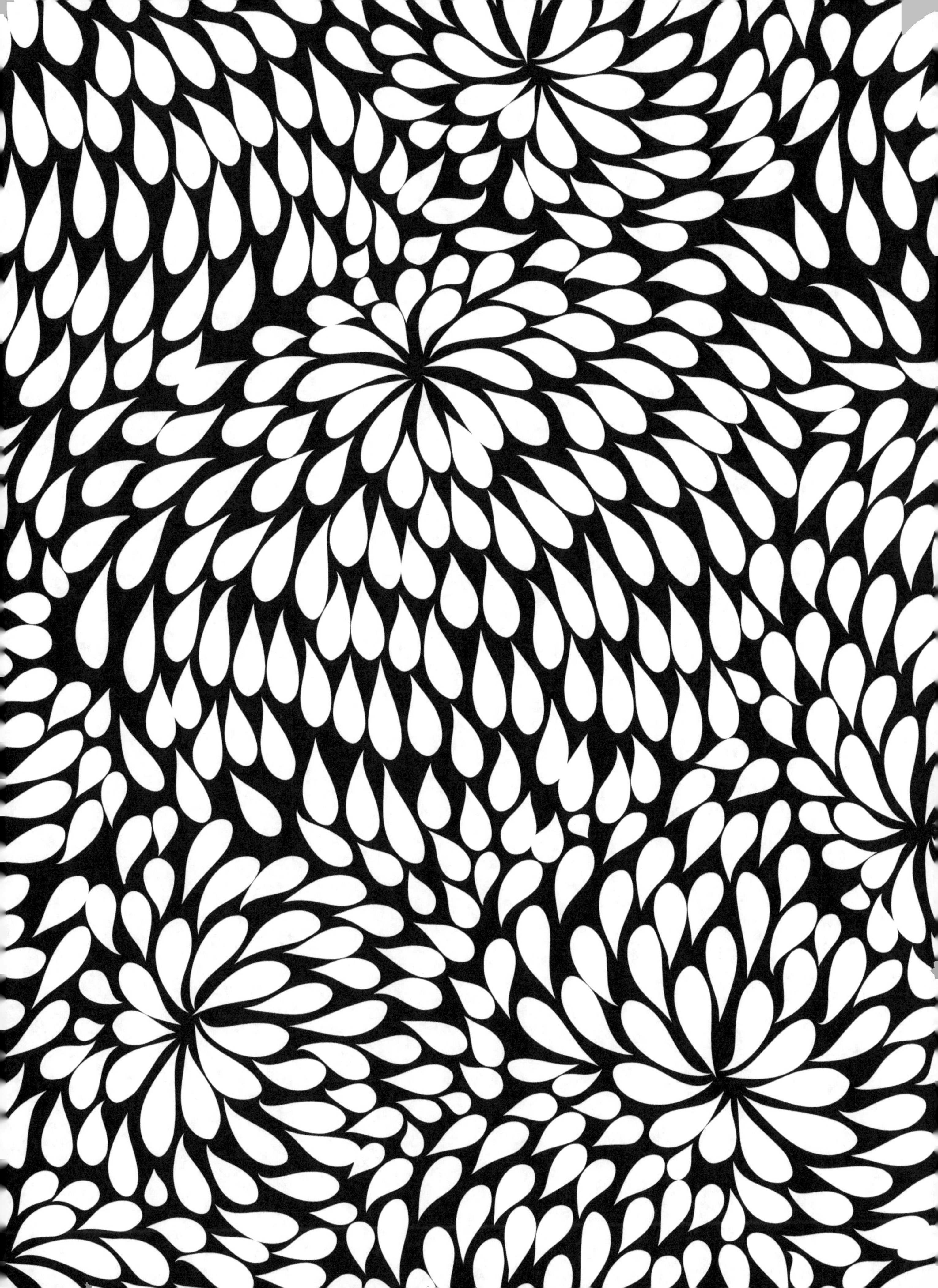

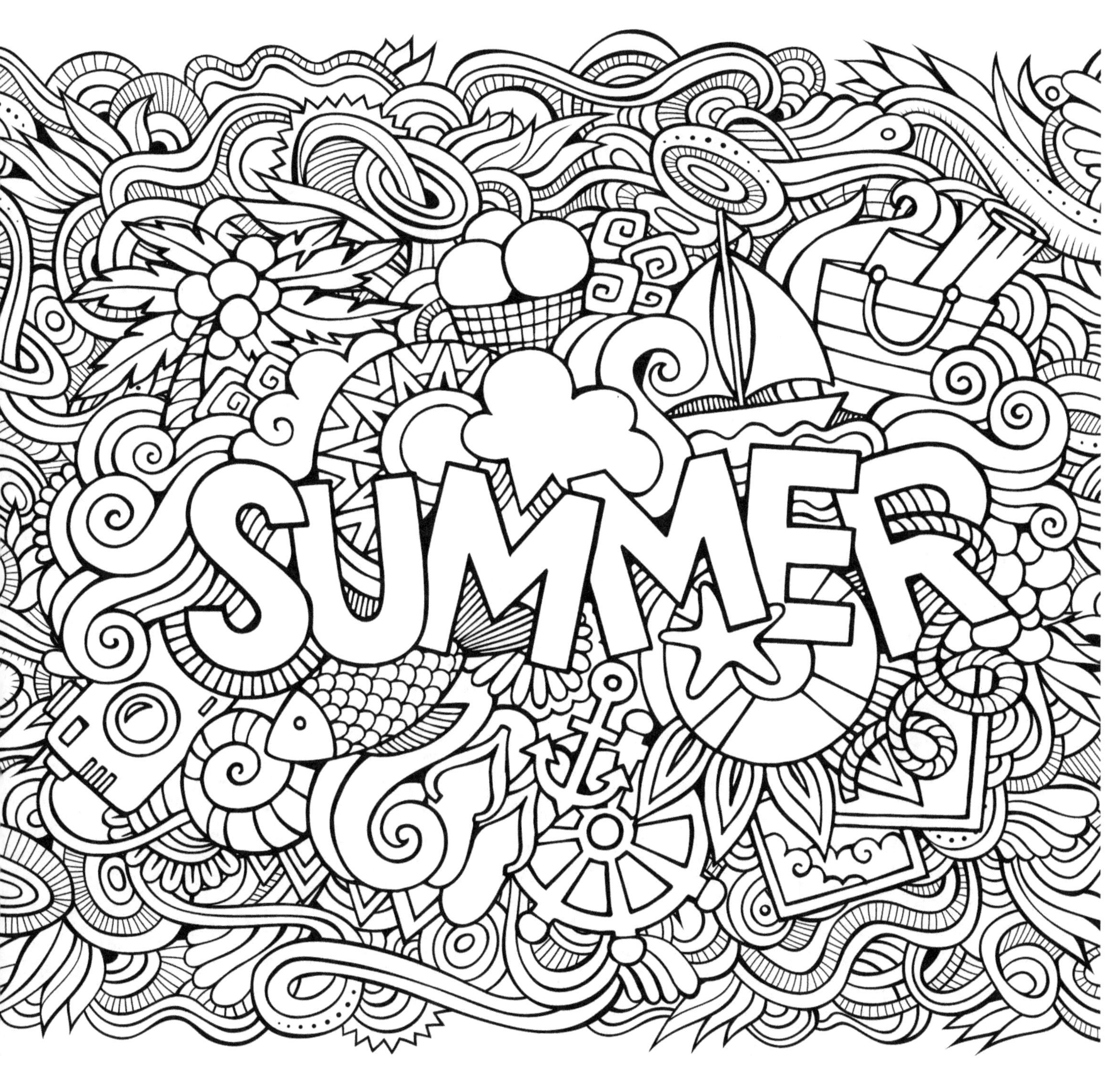
SUMMER

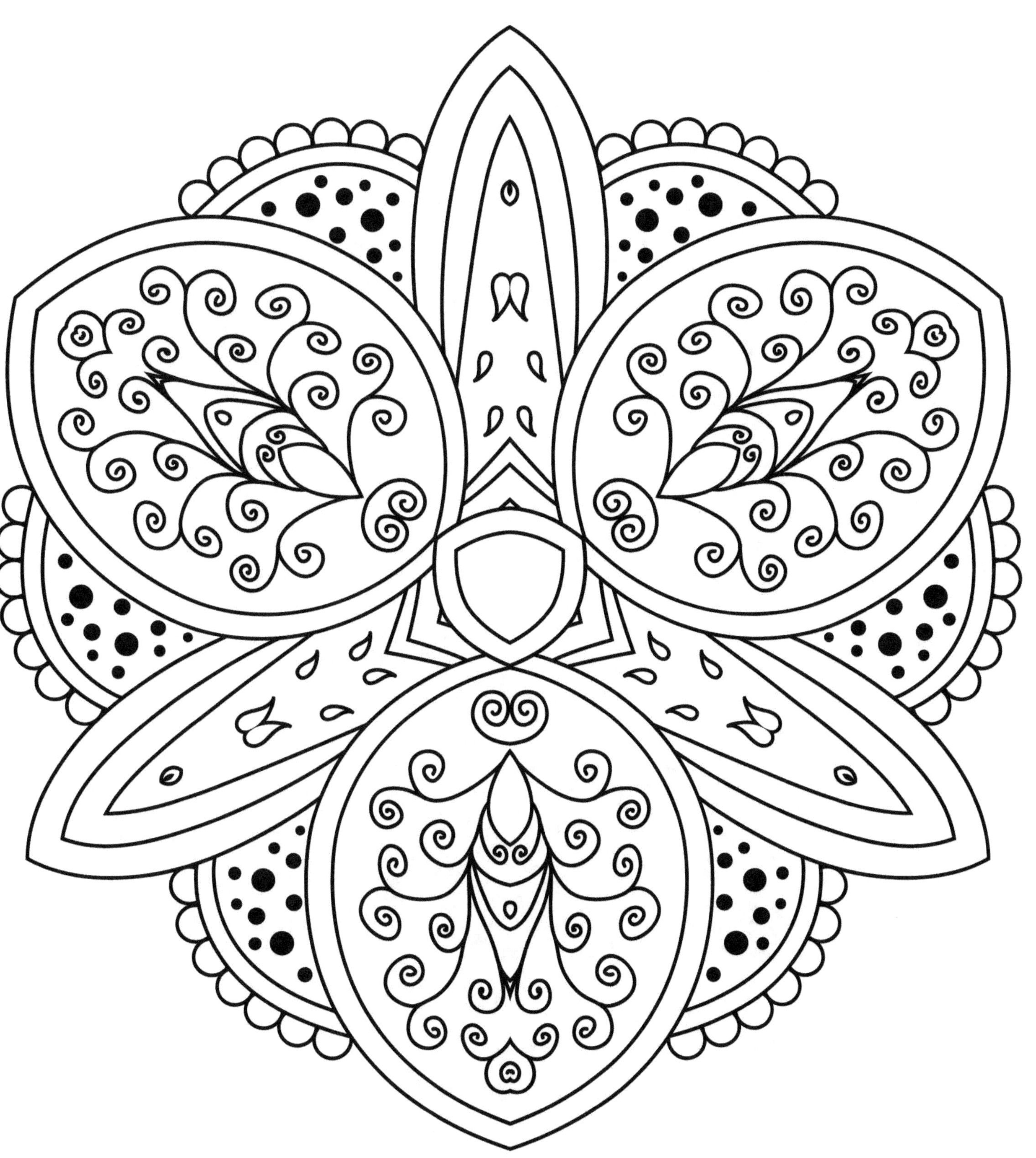

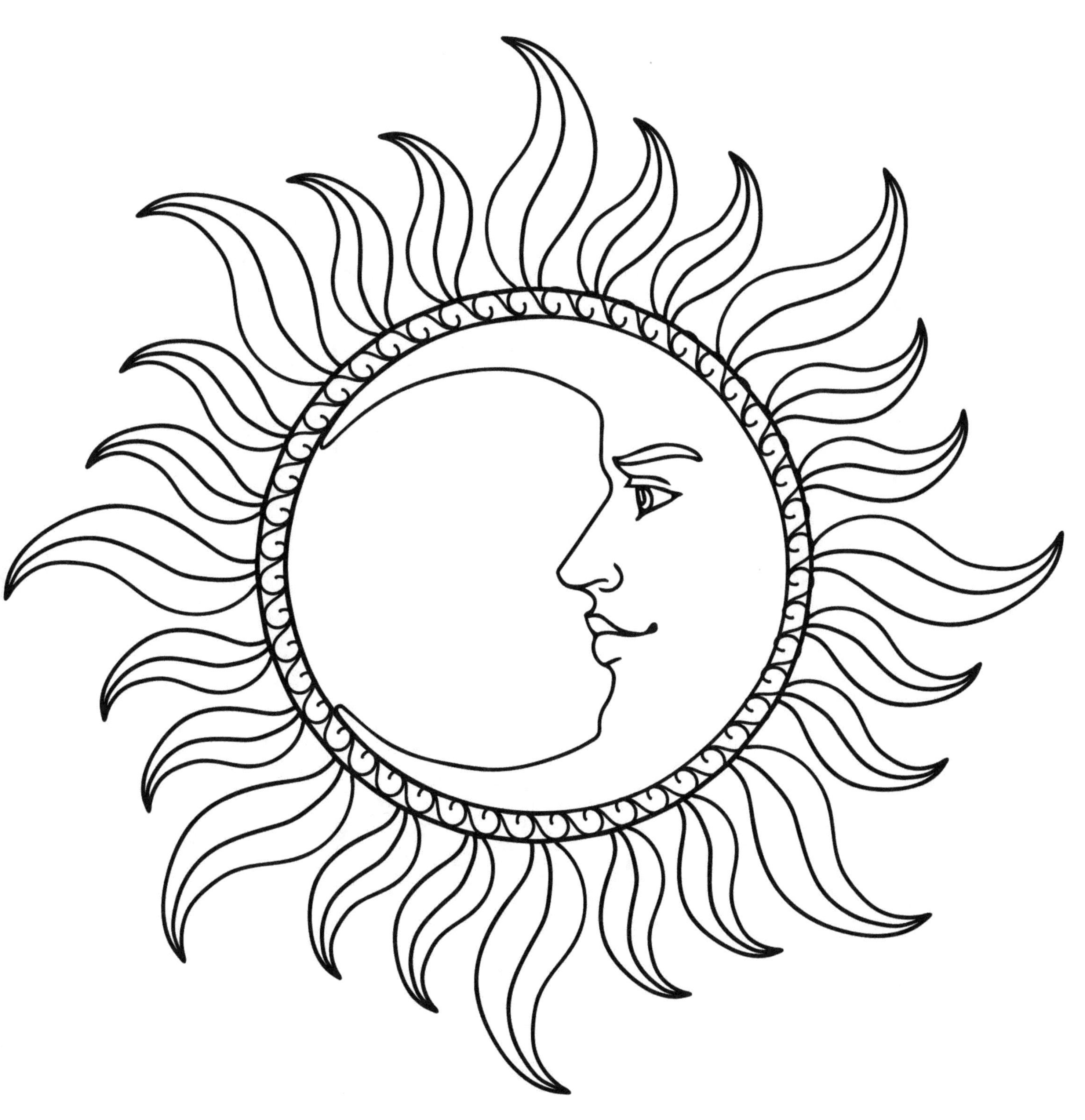

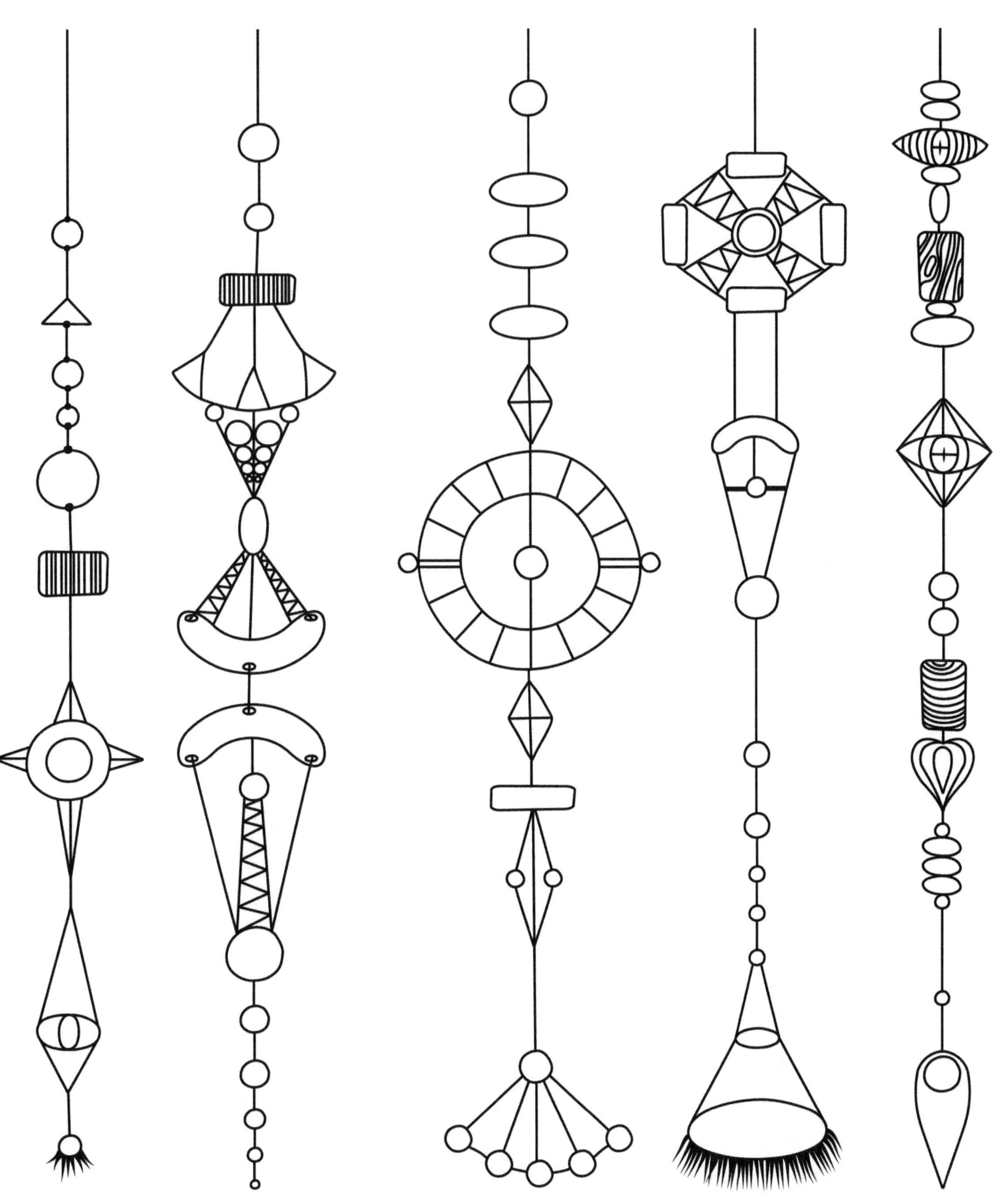

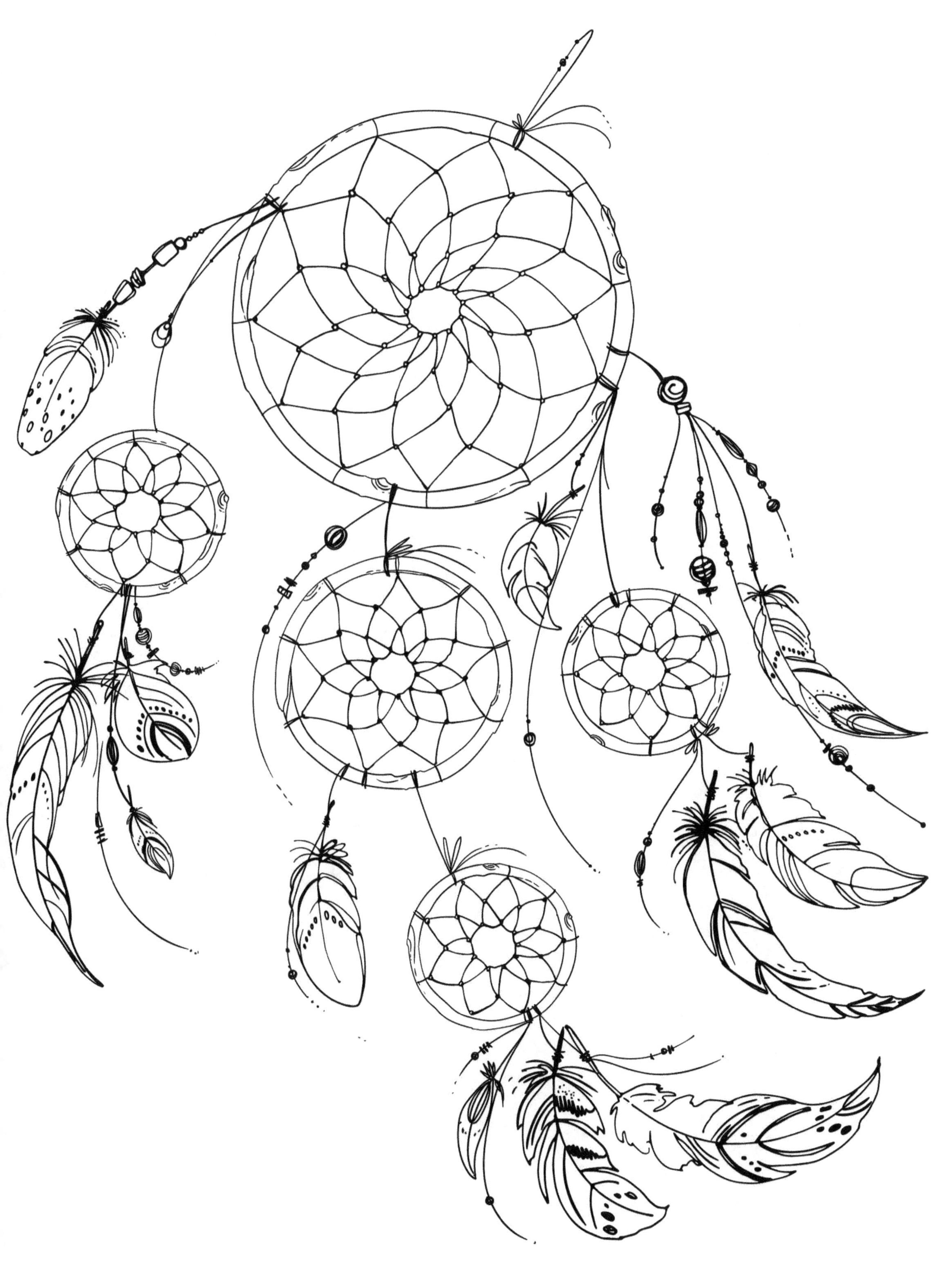

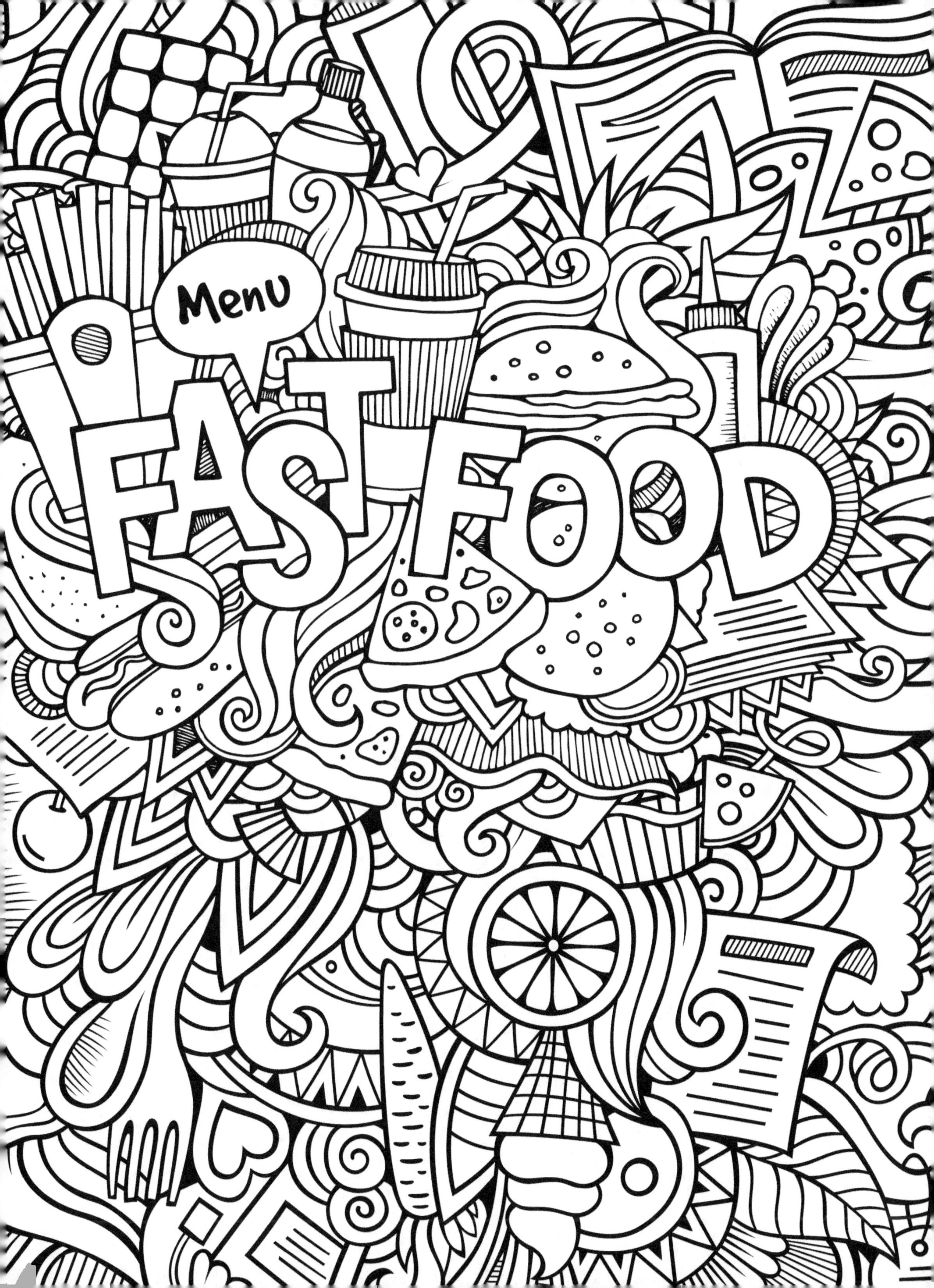
Menu
FAST FOOD

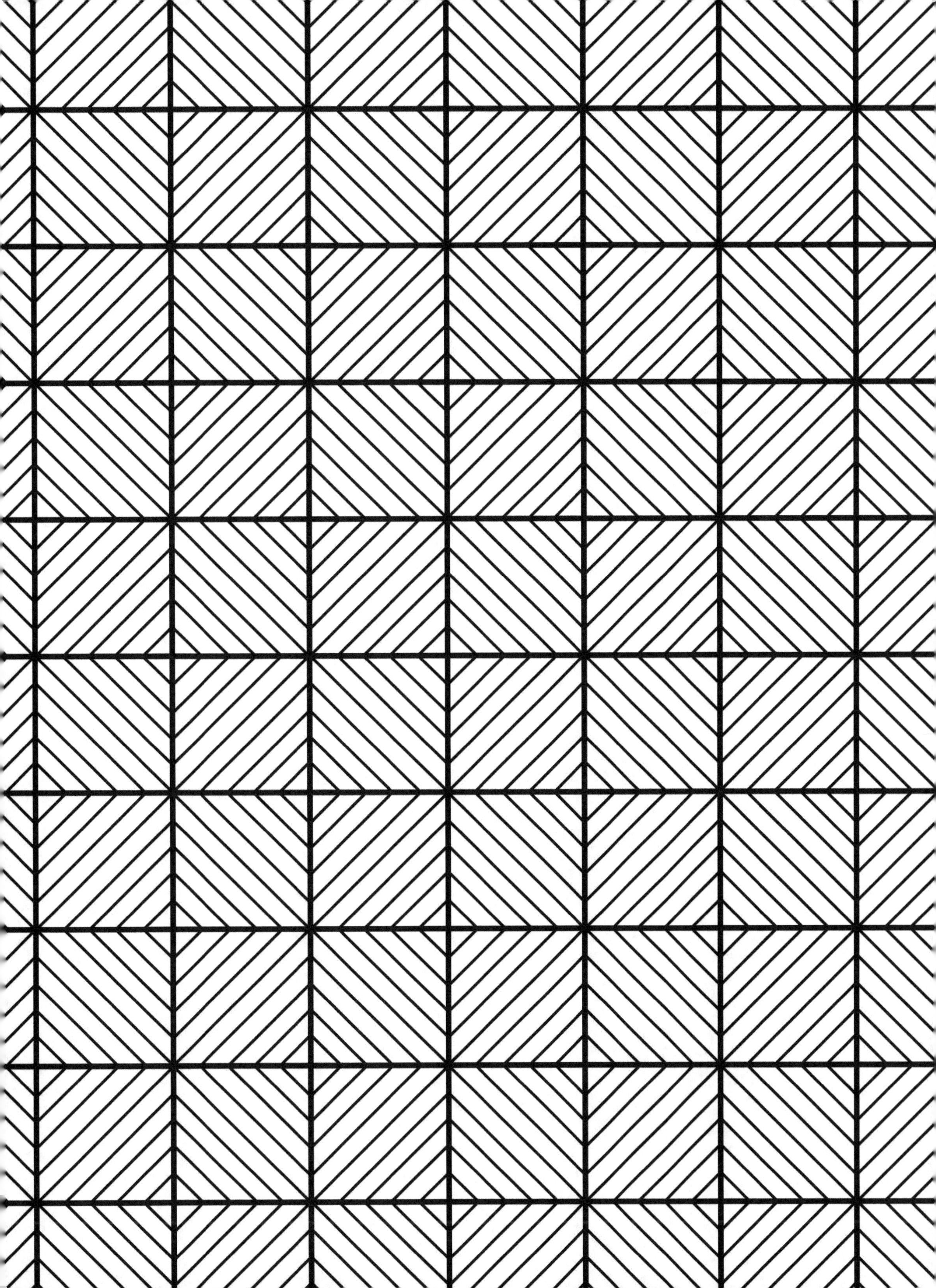

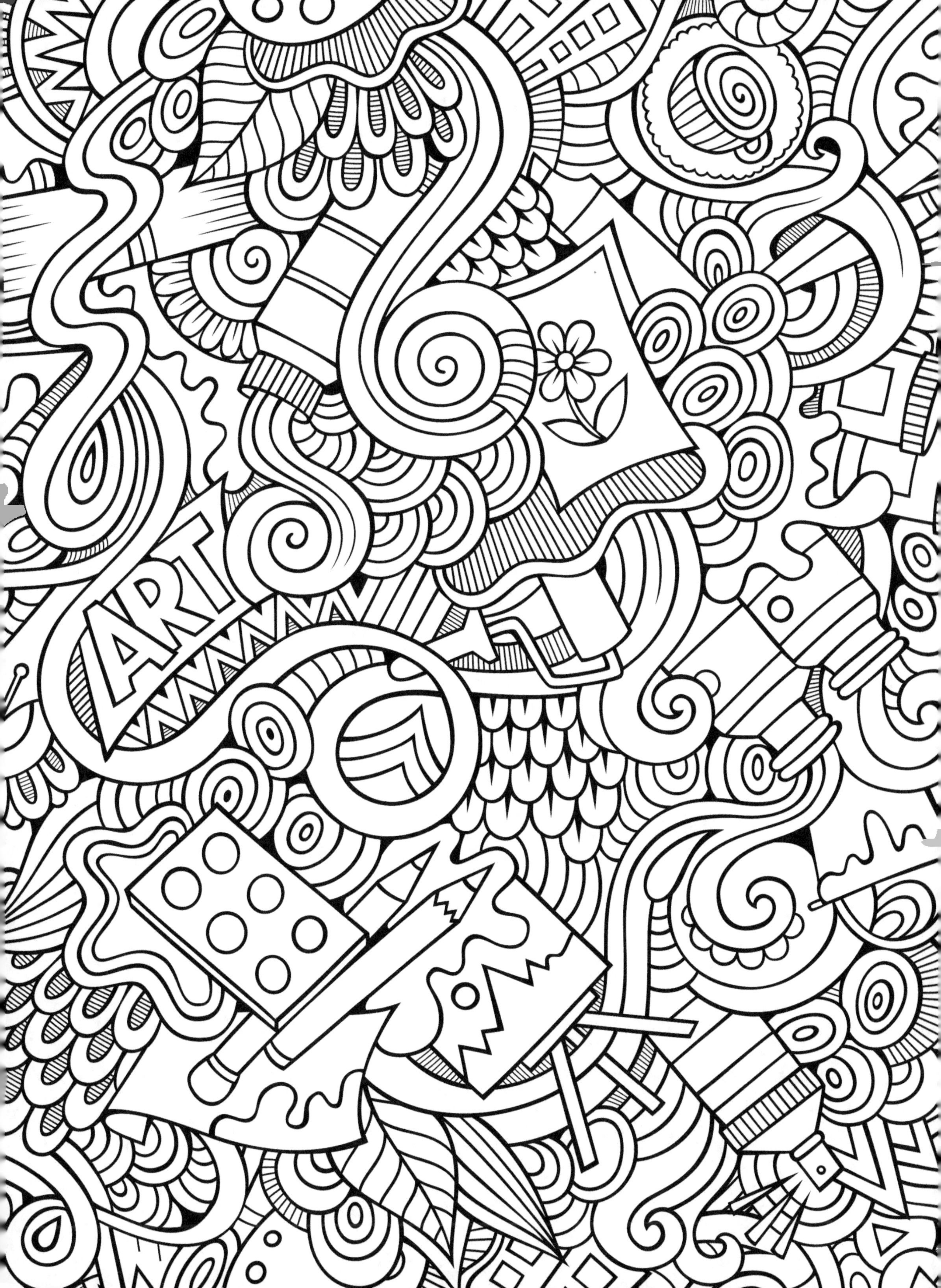
ART

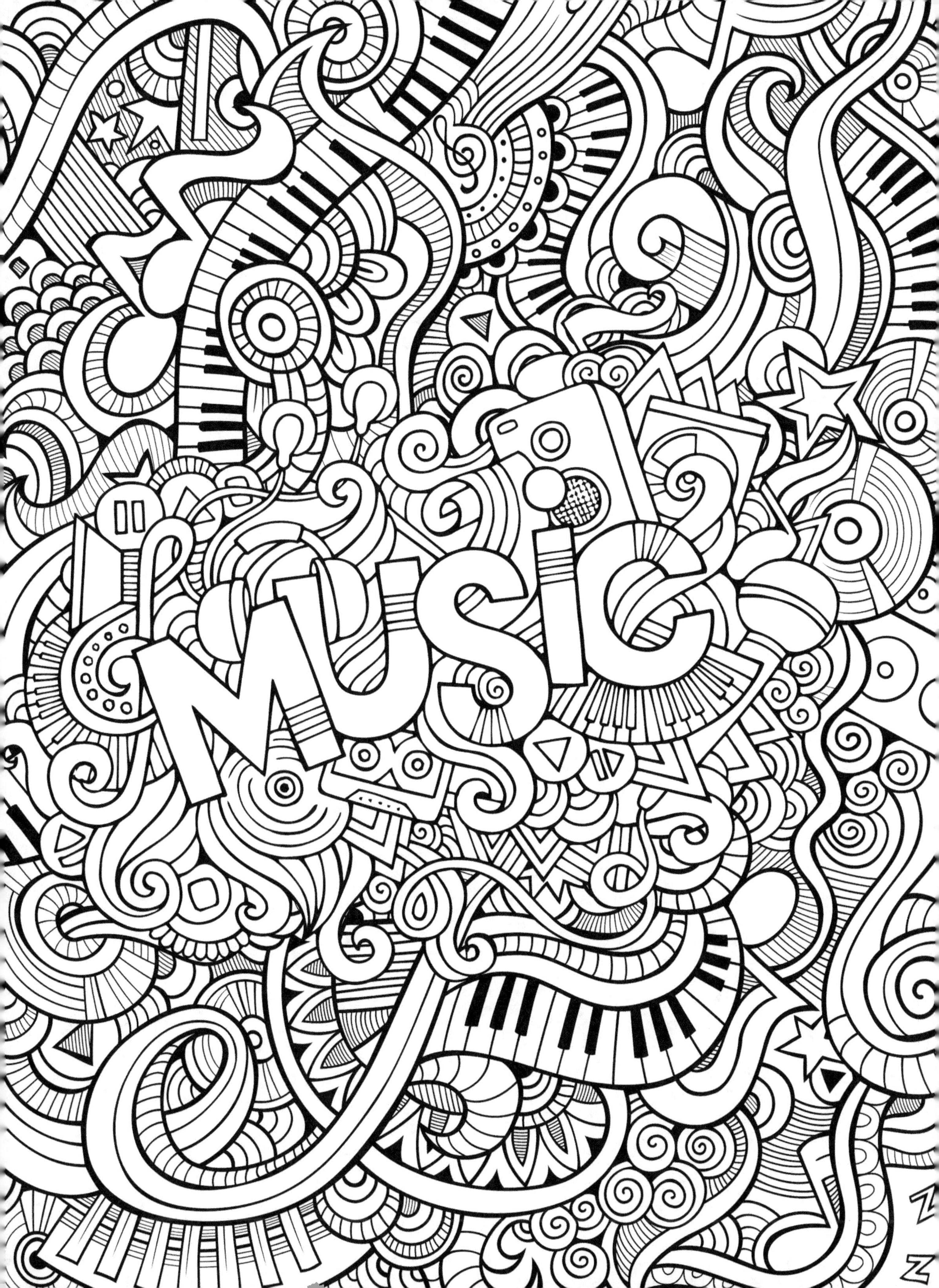
MUSIC

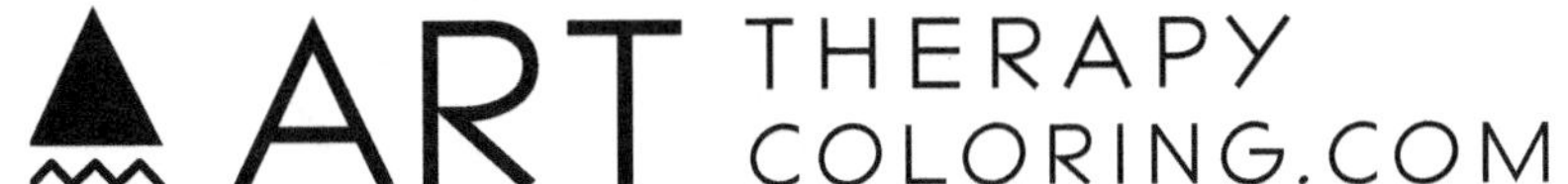

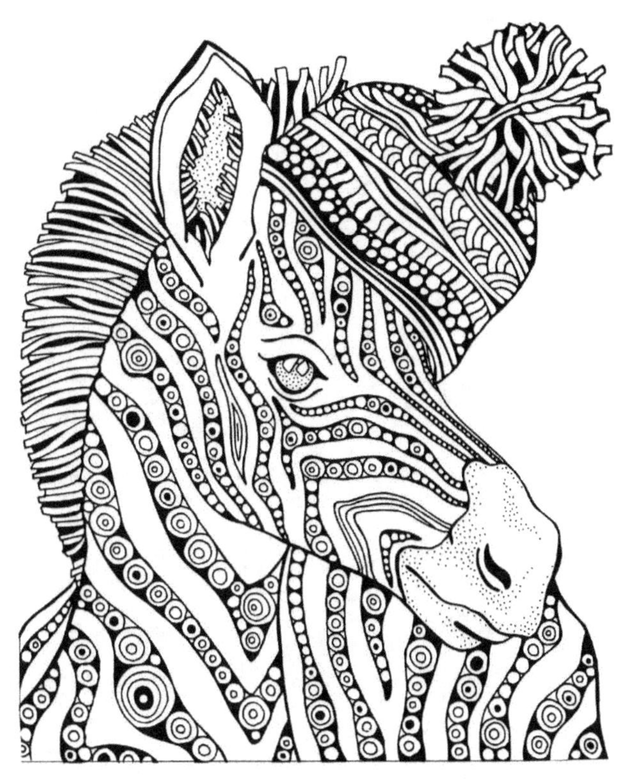

Did You Enjoy Our Coloring Book?

We Want To Hear About It!

Help spread the word about our coloring books! The best way to spread the word is through reviews. We know how busy you are, especially with all of that coloring, but we would appreciate it!

Visit our website at www.arttherapycoloring.com

Over 200 Art Therapy Coloring Books

See our collection of over 200 Art Therapy Coloring Books for Adults, Men, Women, Seniors, Teens, Kids, Boys, and Girls.

Coloring Books For Teens

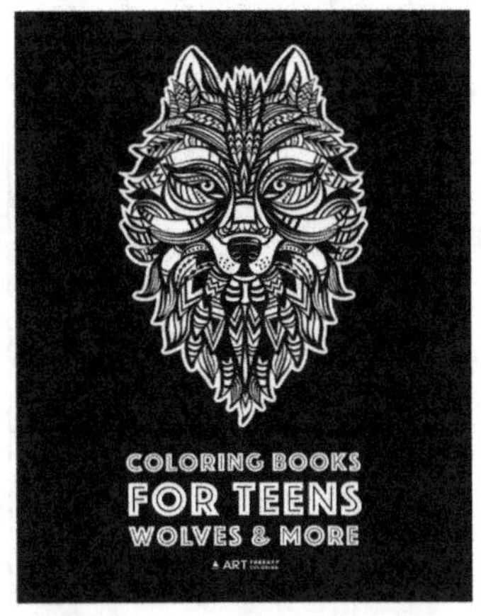

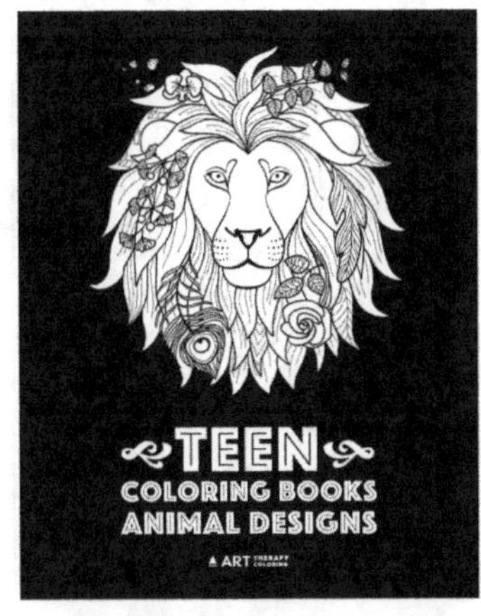

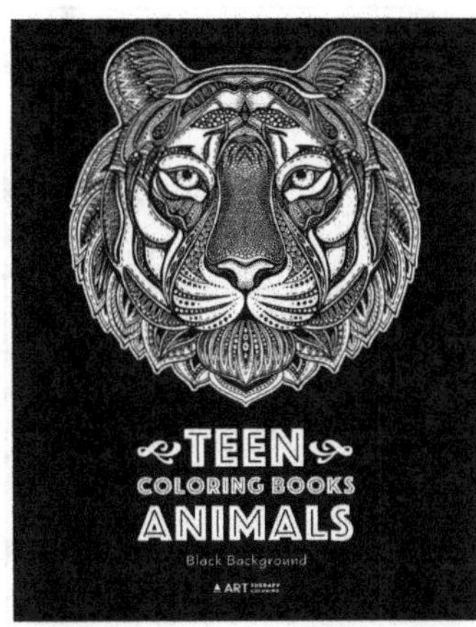

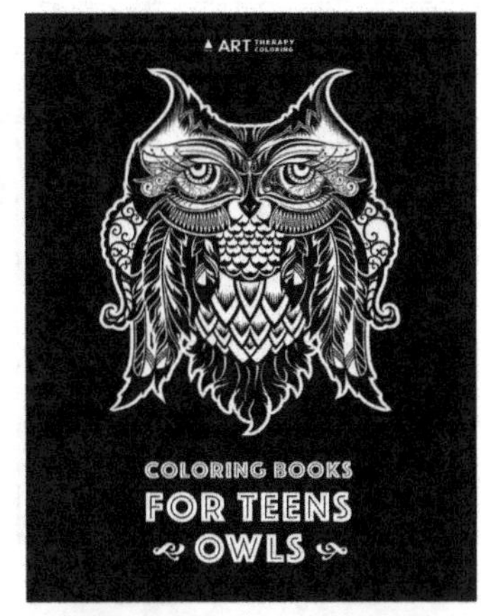

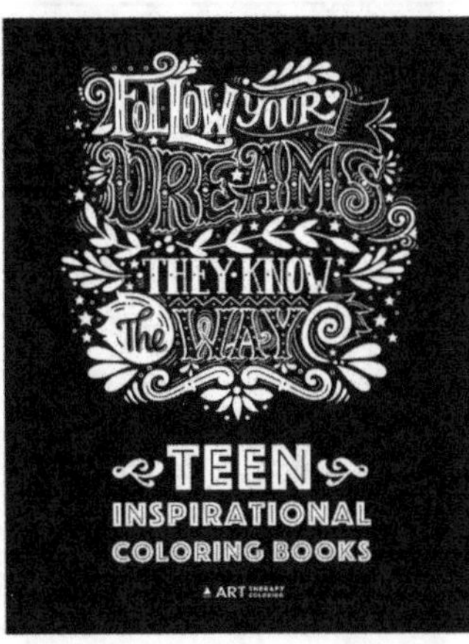

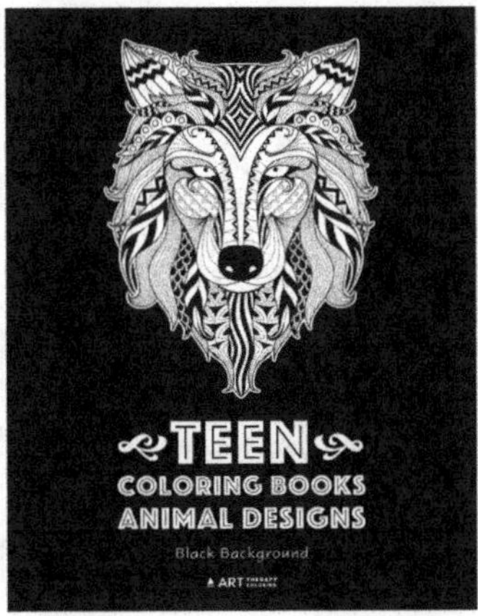

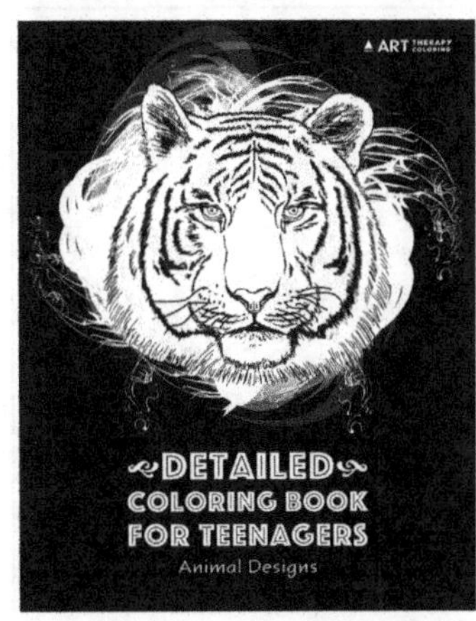

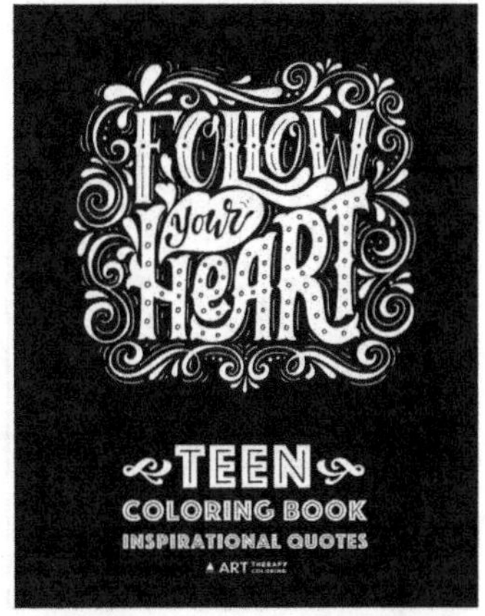

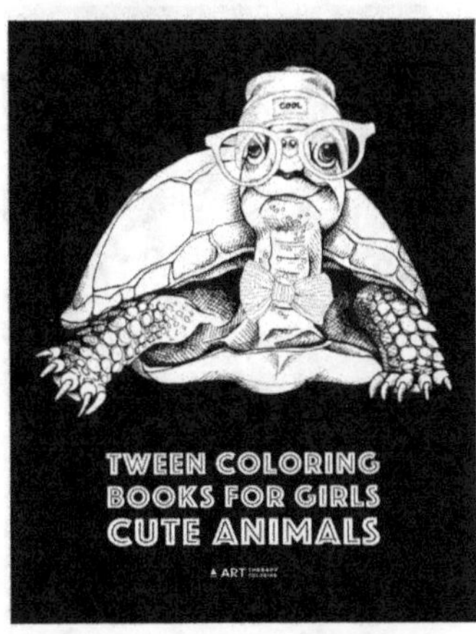

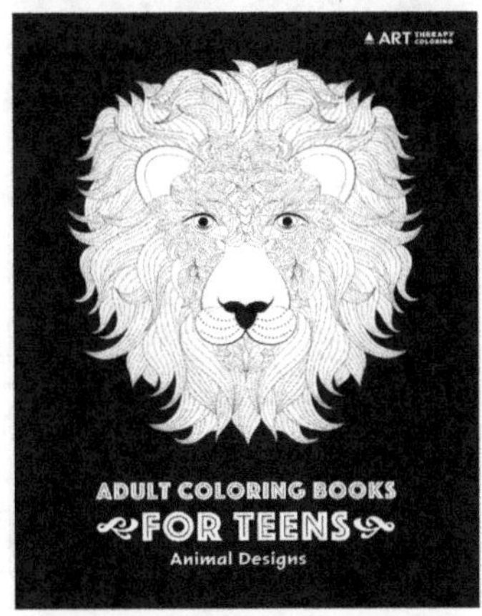

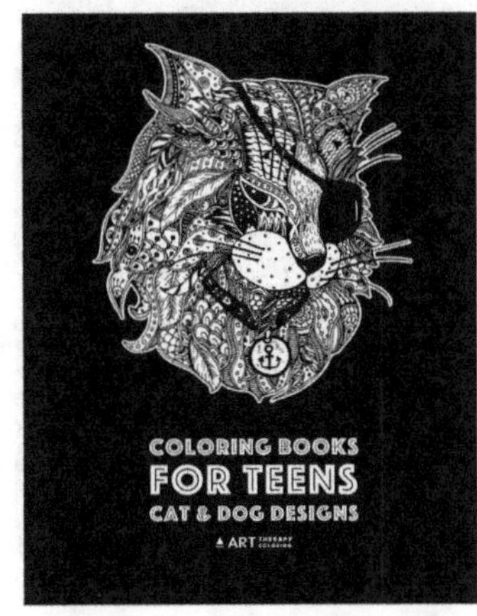

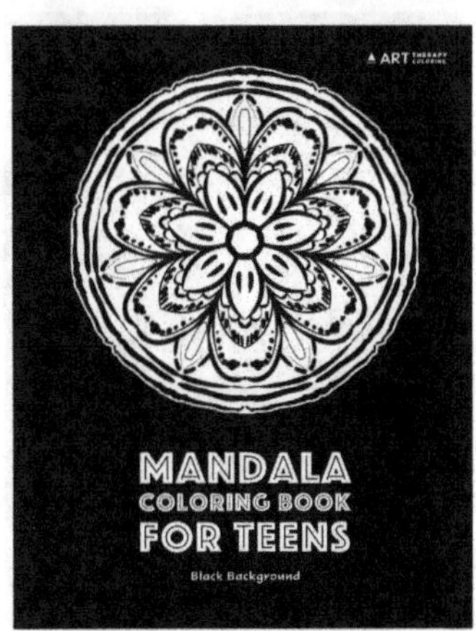

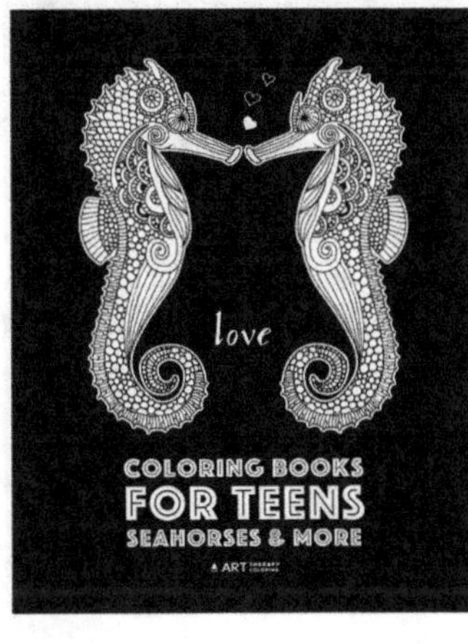

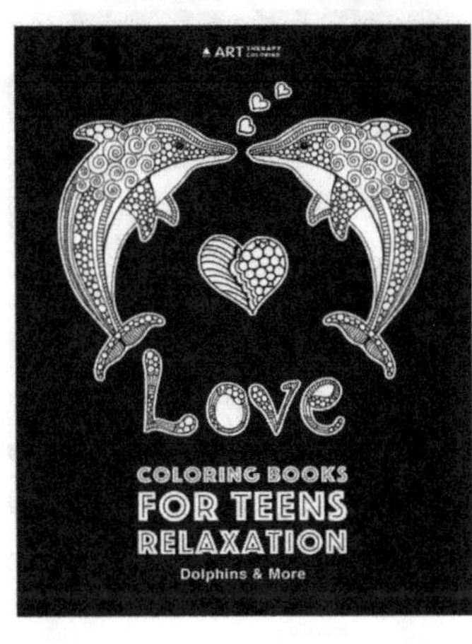

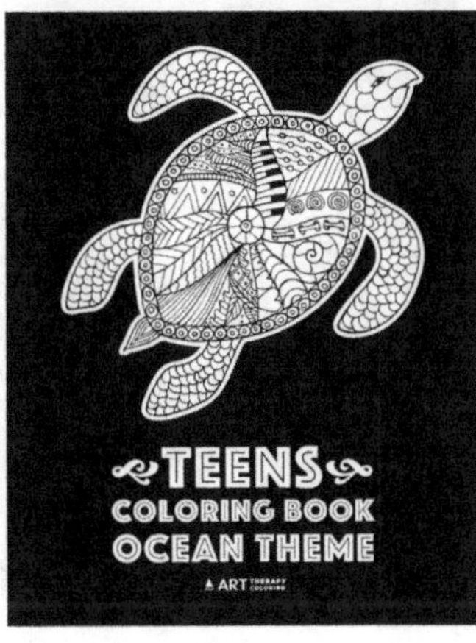

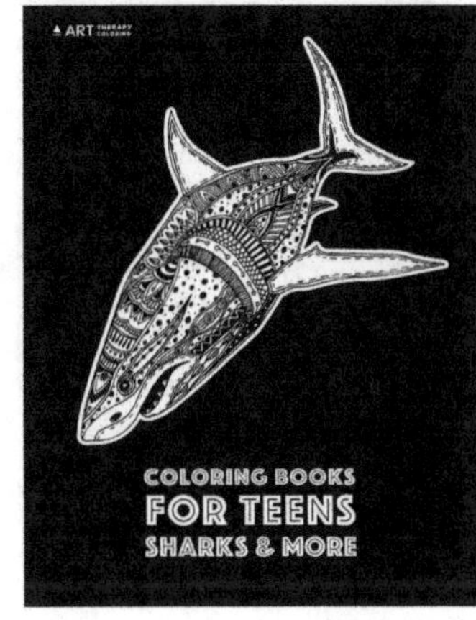

Coloring Books For Teens

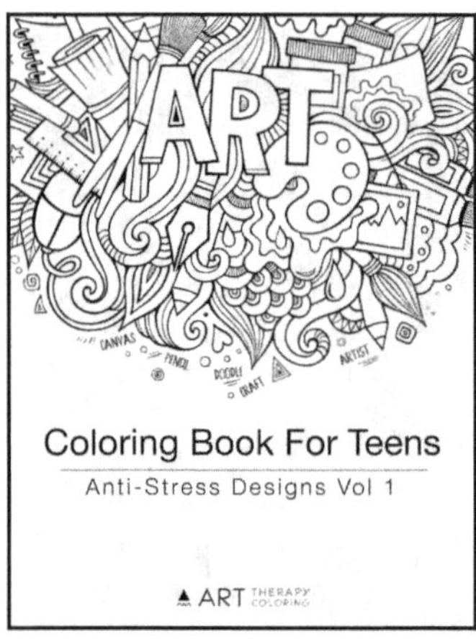

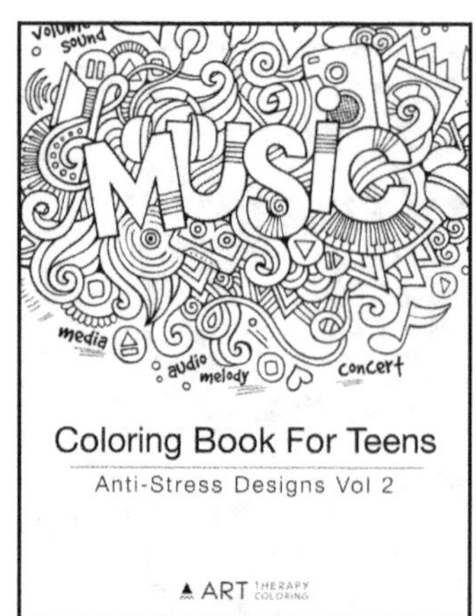

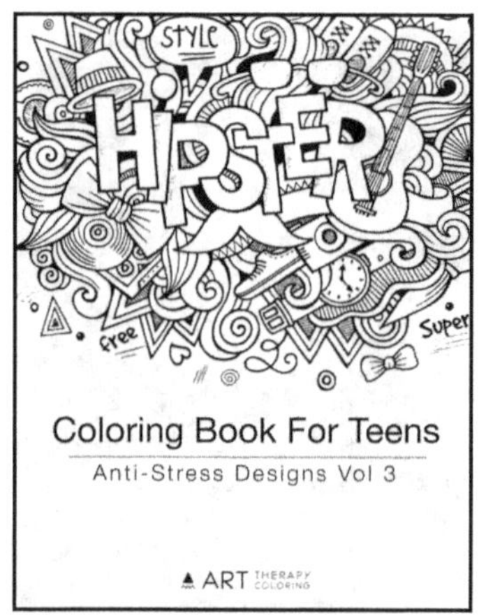

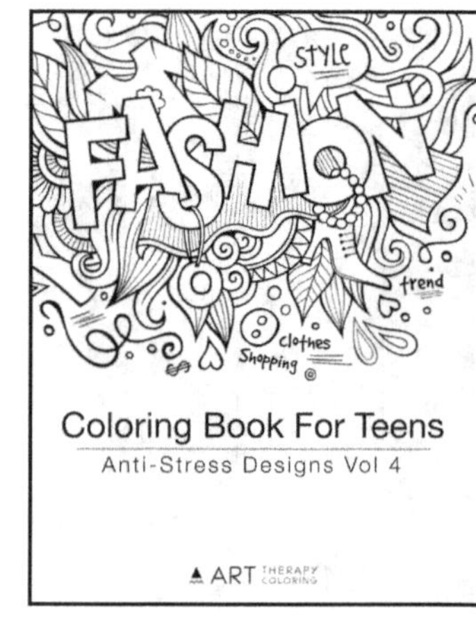

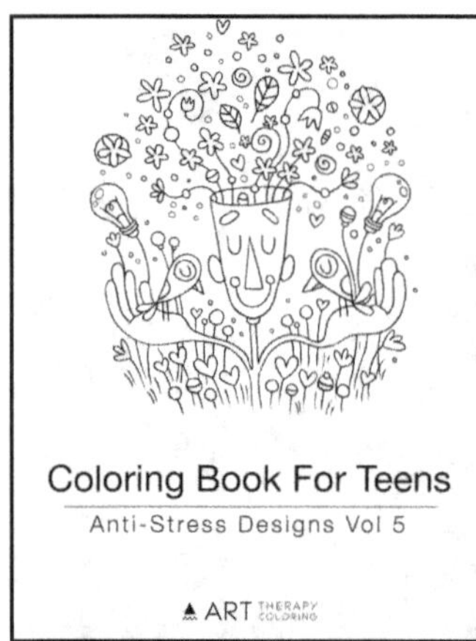

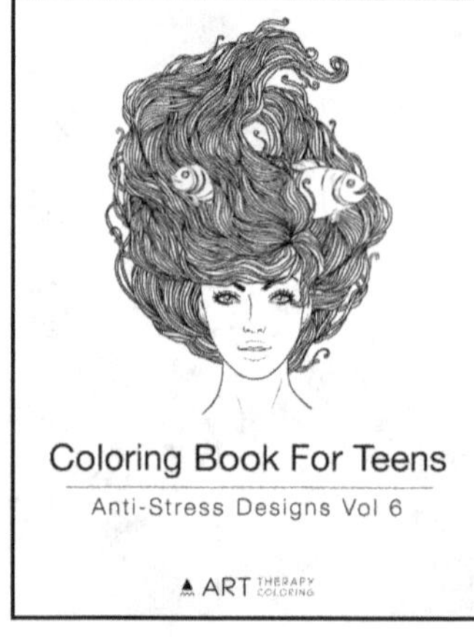

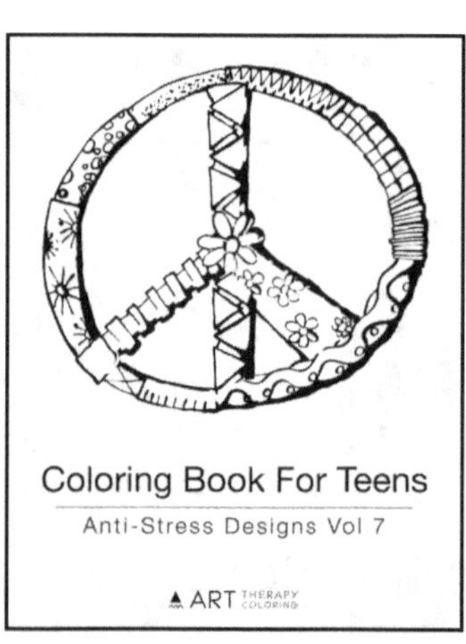

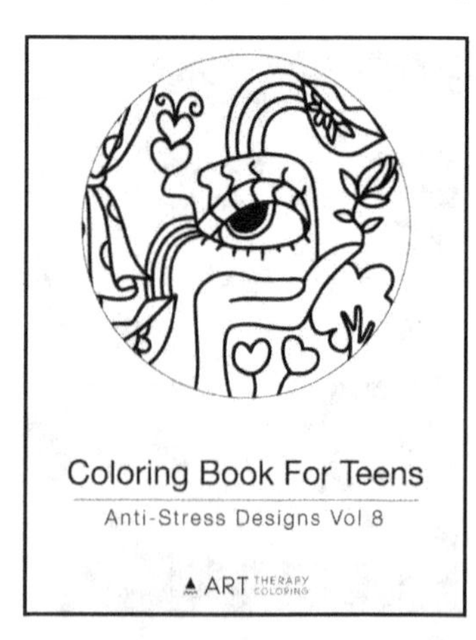

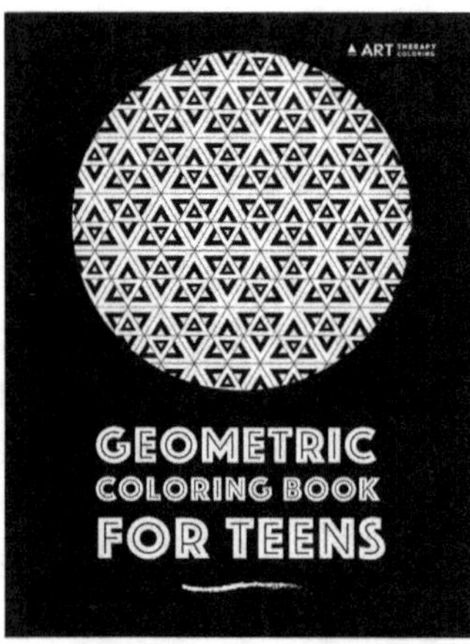

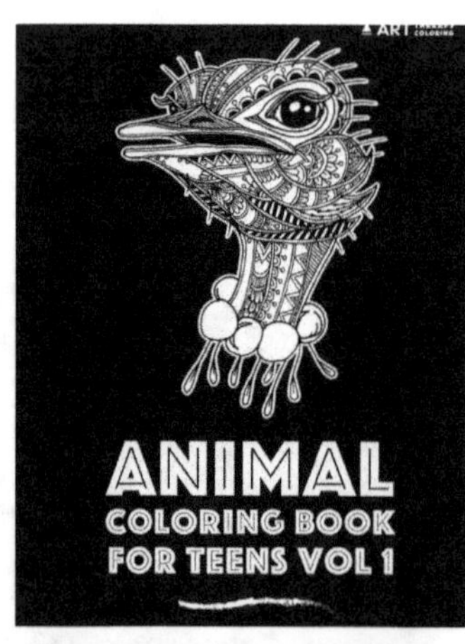

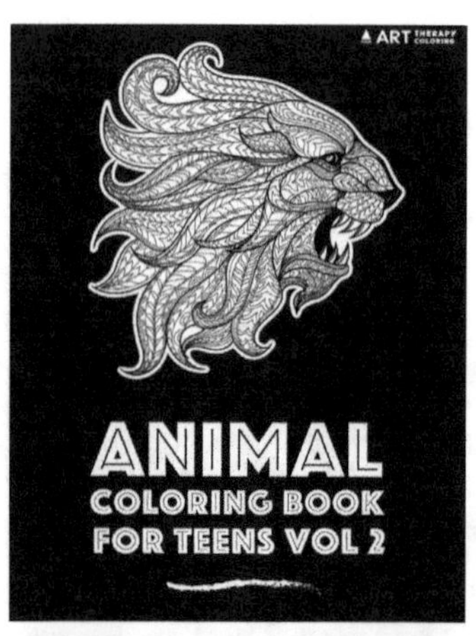

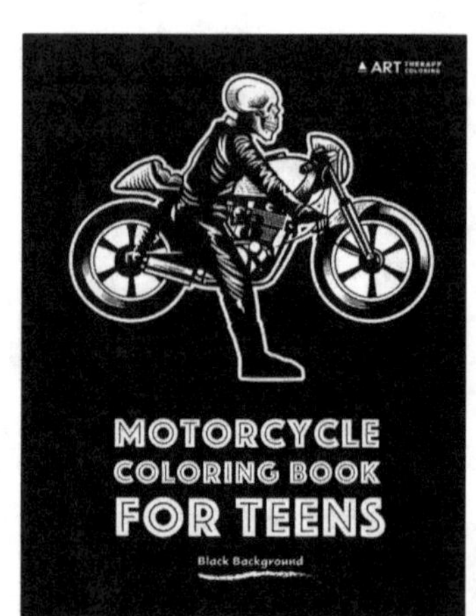

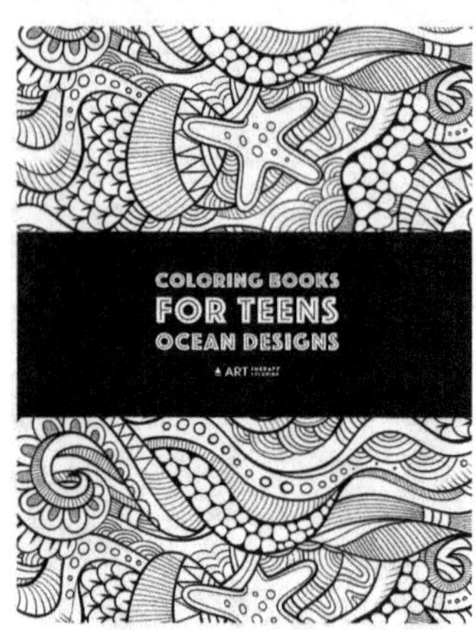

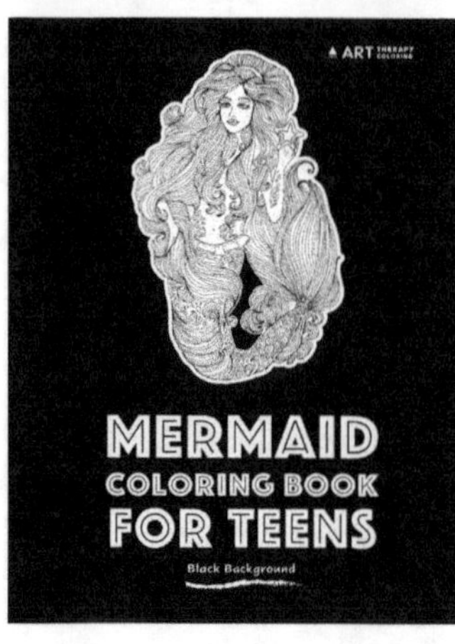

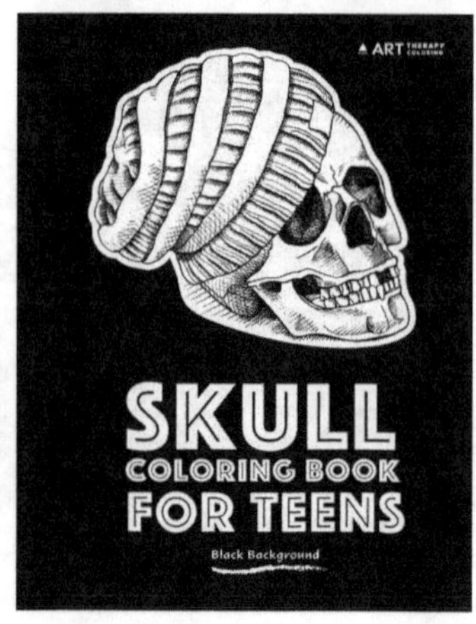

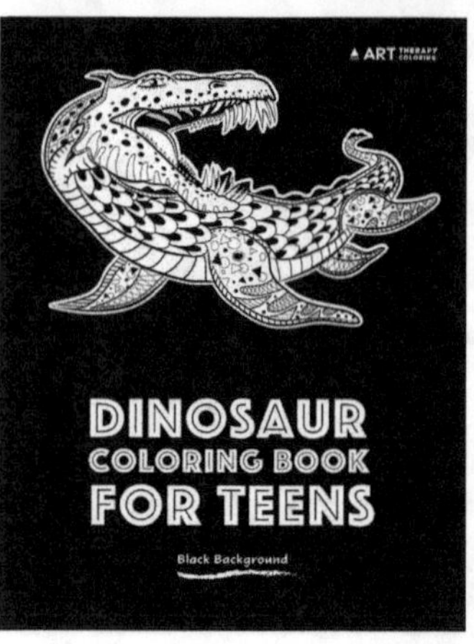

Coloring Books For Girls

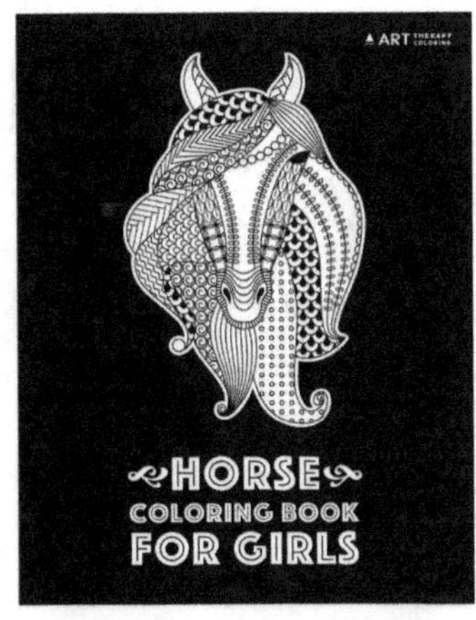
HORSE
COLORING BOOK
FOR GIRLS

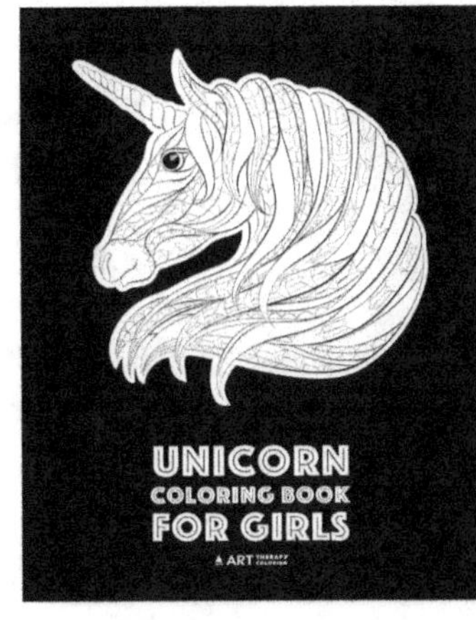
UNICORN
COLORING BOOK
FOR GIRLS

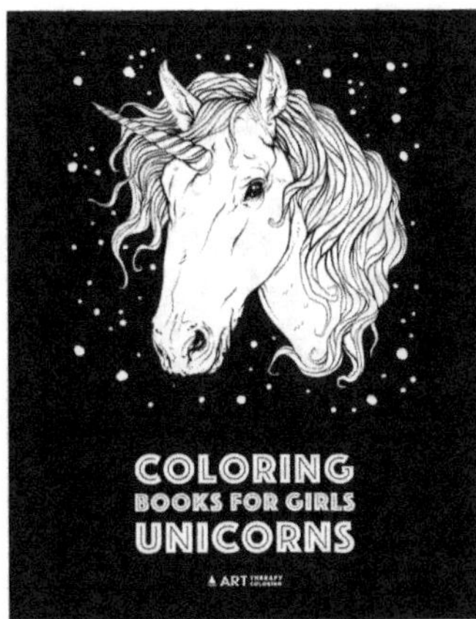
COLORING
BOOKS FOR GIRLS
UNICORNS

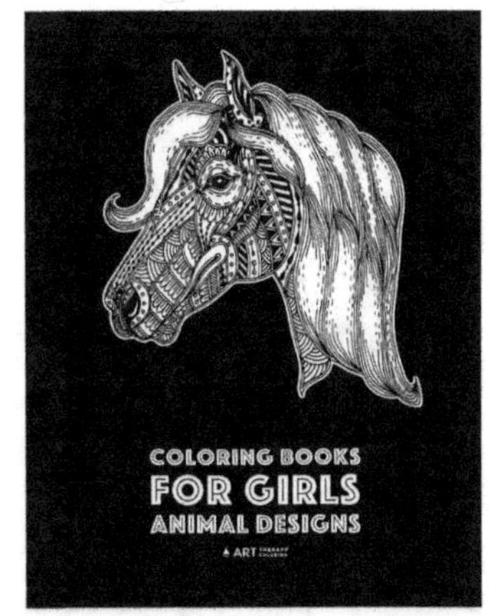
COLORING BOOKS
FOR GIRLS
ANIMAL DESIGNS

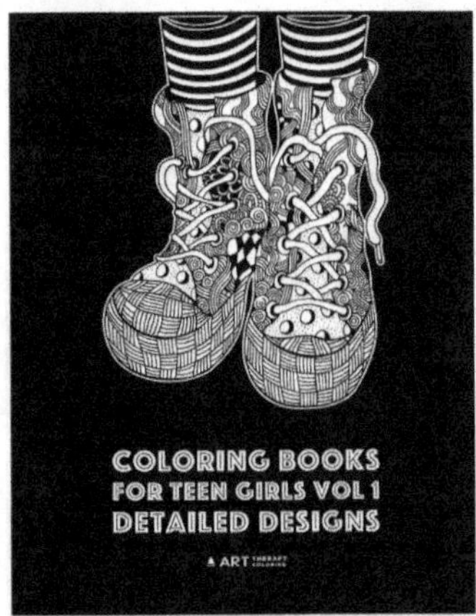
COLORING BOOKS
FOR TEEN GIRLS VOL 1
DETAILED DESIGNS

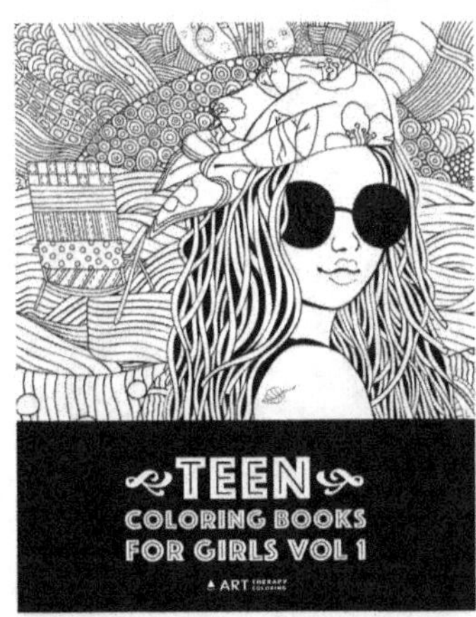
TEEN
COLORING BOOKS
FOR GIRLS VOL 1

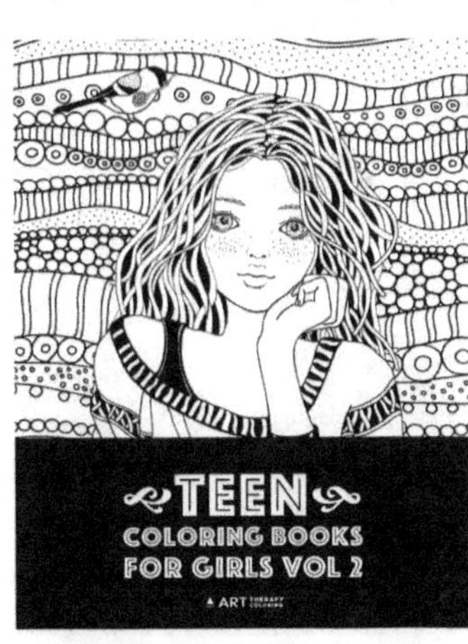
TEEN
COLORING BOOKS
FOR GIRLS VOL 2

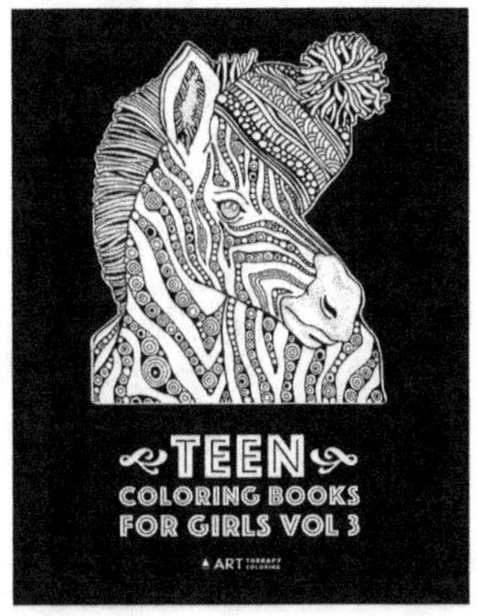
TEEN
COLORING BOOKS
FOR GIRLS VOL 3

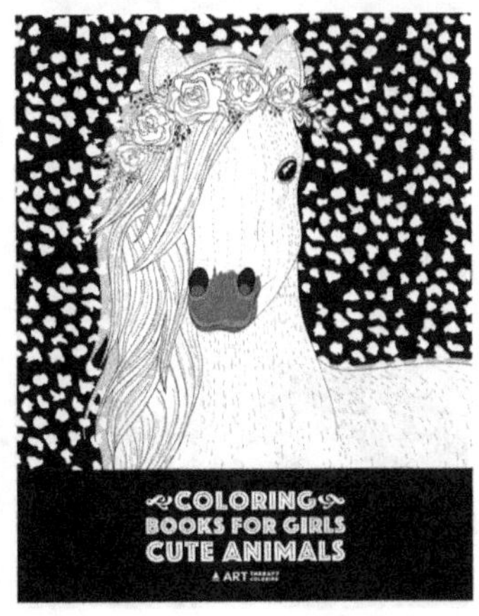
COLORING
BOOKS FOR GIRLS
CUTE ANIMALS

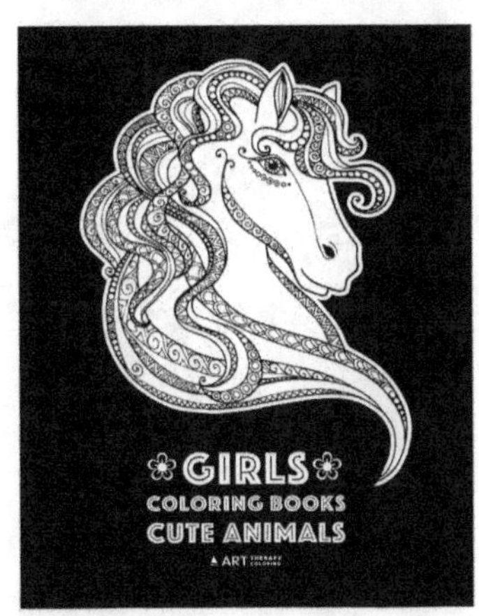
GIRLS
COLORING BOOKS
CUTE ANIMALS

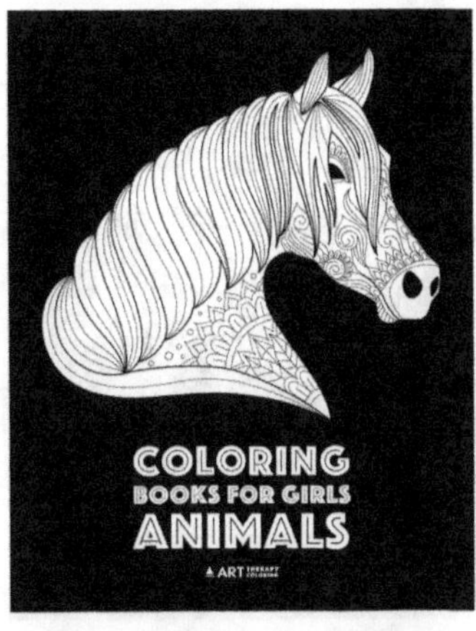
COLORING
BOOKS FOR GIRLS
ANIMALS

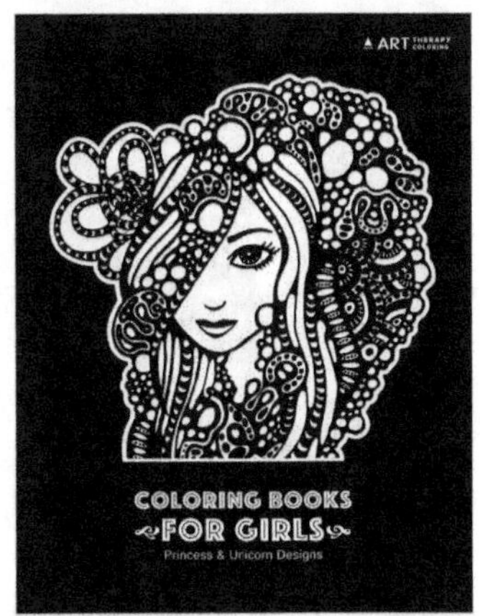
COLORING BOOKS
FOR GIRLS
Princess & Unicorn Designs

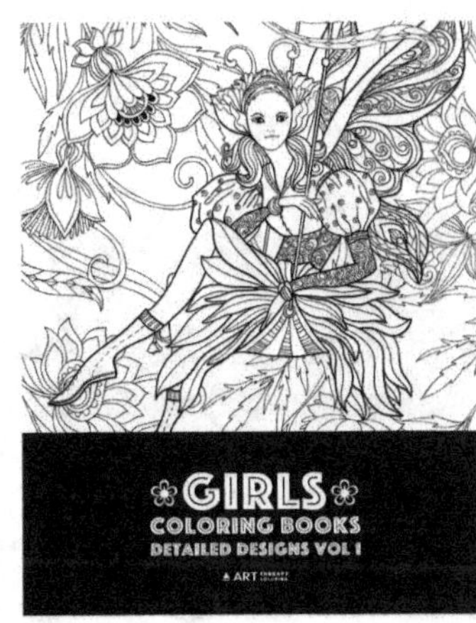
GIRLS
COLORING BOOKS
DETAILED DESIGNS VOL 1

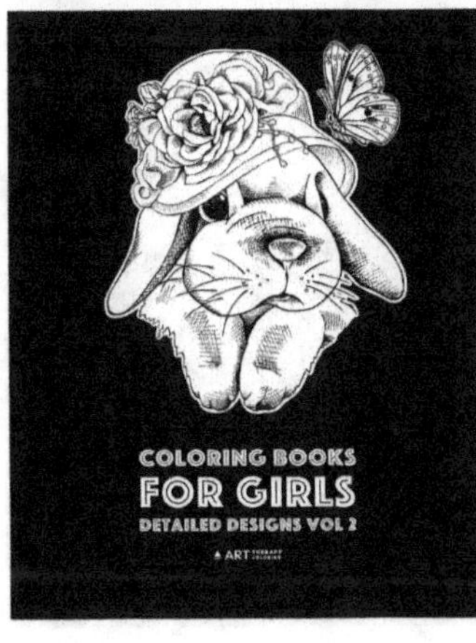
COLORING BOOKS
FOR GIRLS
DETAILED DESIGNS VOL 2

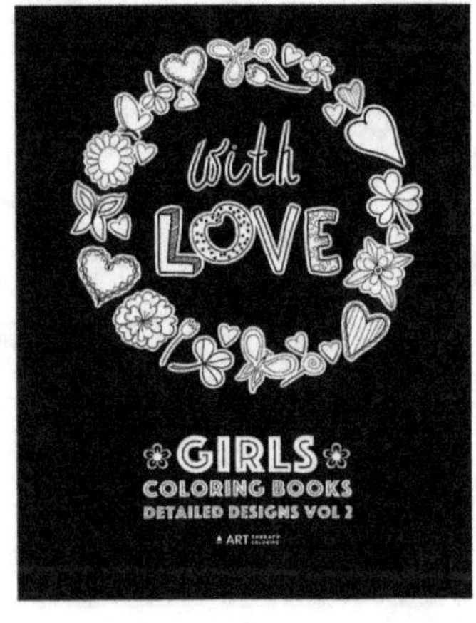
With
LOVE
GIRLS
COLORING BOOKS
DETAILED DESIGNS VOL 2

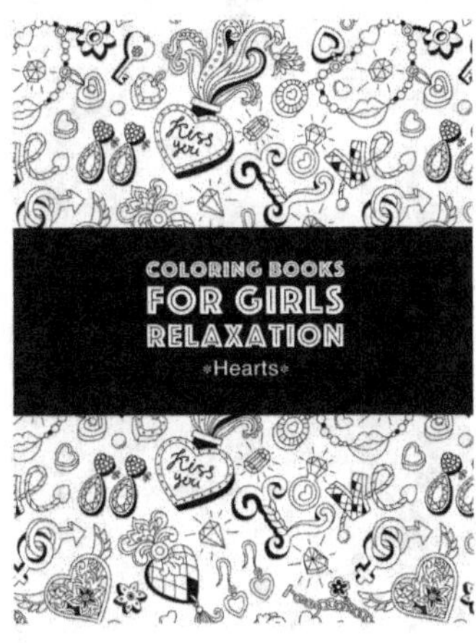
COLORING BOOKS
FOR GIRLS
RELAXATION
Hearts

Coloring Books For Boys

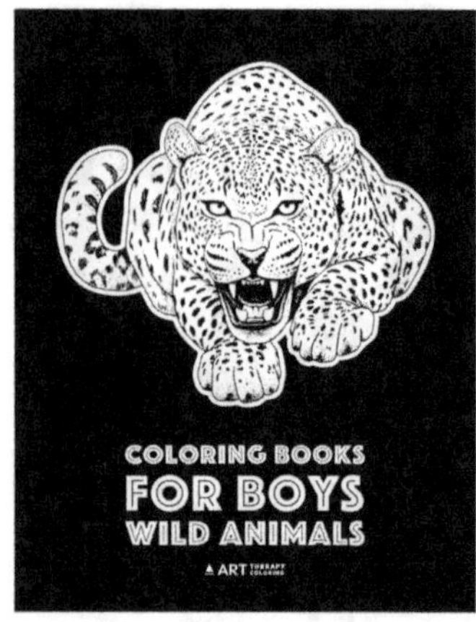
COLORING BOOKS
FOR BOYS
WILD ANIMALS
ART THERAPY COLORING

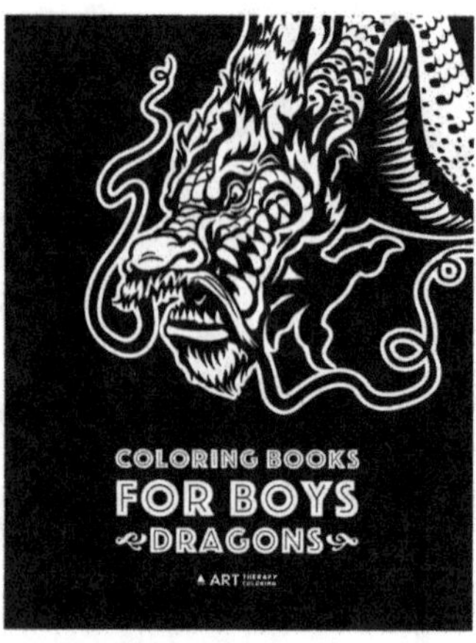
COLORING BOOKS
FOR BOYS
DRAGONS
ART THERAPY COLORING

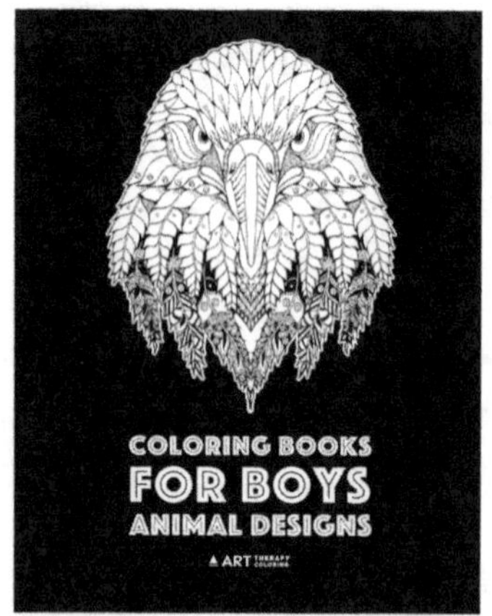
COLORING BOOKS
FOR BOYS
ANIMAL DESIGNS
ART THERAPY COLORING

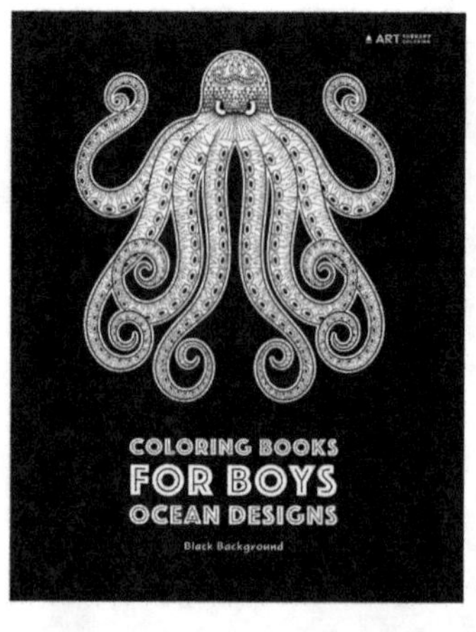
ART THERAPY COLORING
COLORING BOOKS
FOR BOYS
OCEAN DESIGNS
Black Background

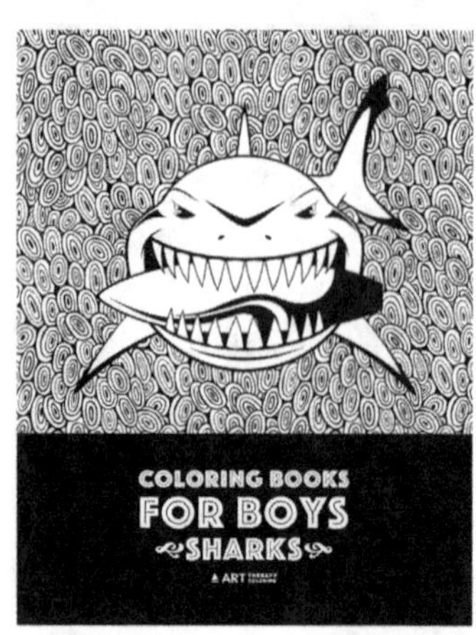
COLORING BOOKS
FOR BOYS
SHARKS
ART THERAPY COLORING

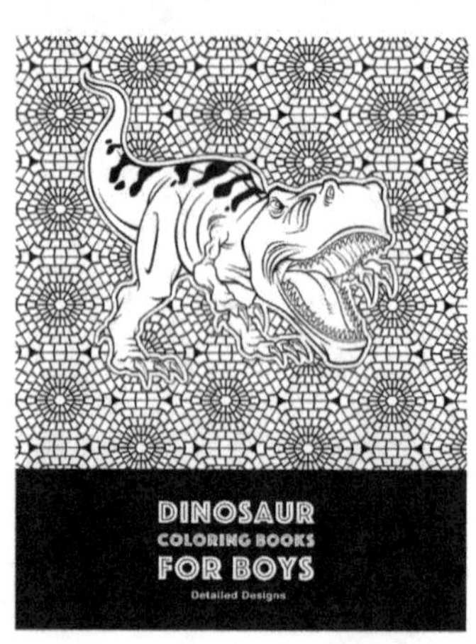
DINOSAUR
COLORING BOOKS
FOR BOYS
Detailed Designs

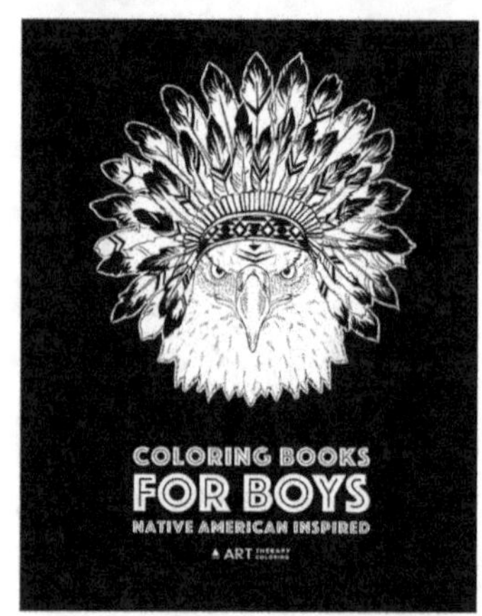
COLORING BOOKS
FOR BOYS
NATIVE AMERICAN INSPIRED
ART THERAPY COLORING

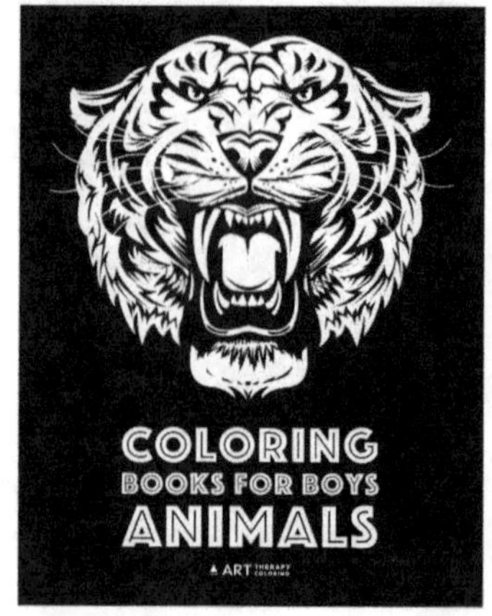
COLORING
BOOKS FOR BOYS
ANIMALS
ART THERAPY COLORING

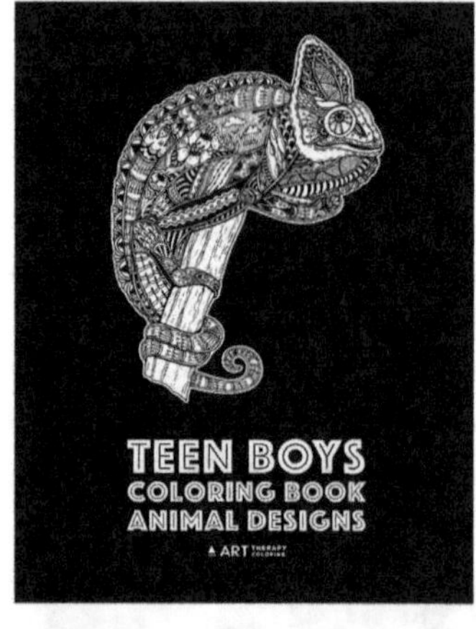
TEEN BOYS
COLORING BOOK
ANIMAL DESIGNS
ART THERAPY COLORING

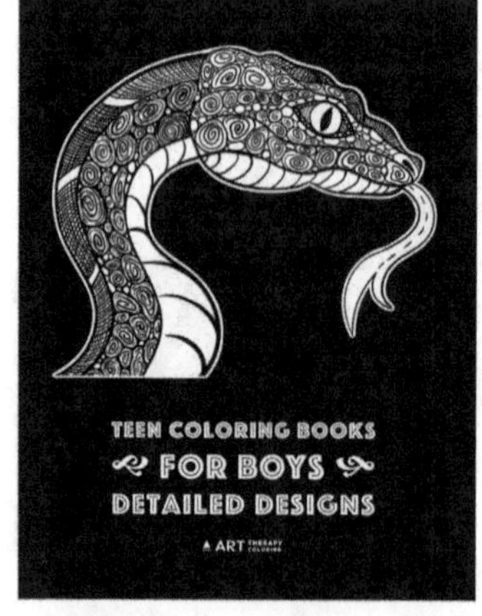
TEEN COLORING BOOKS
FOR BOYS
DETAILED DESIGNS
ART THERAPY COLORING

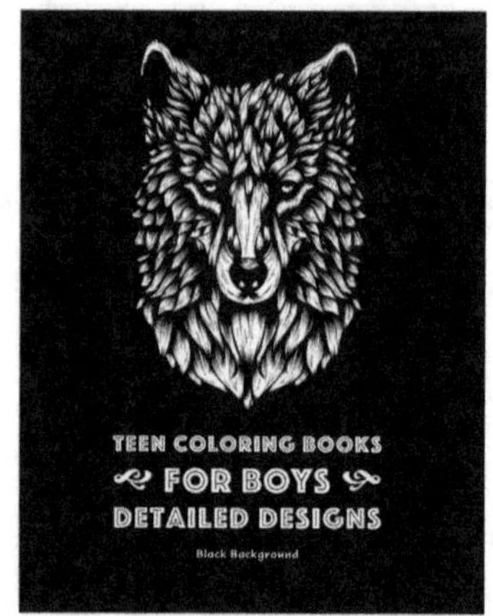
TEEN COLORING BOOKS
FOR BOYS
DETAILED DESIGNS
Black Background

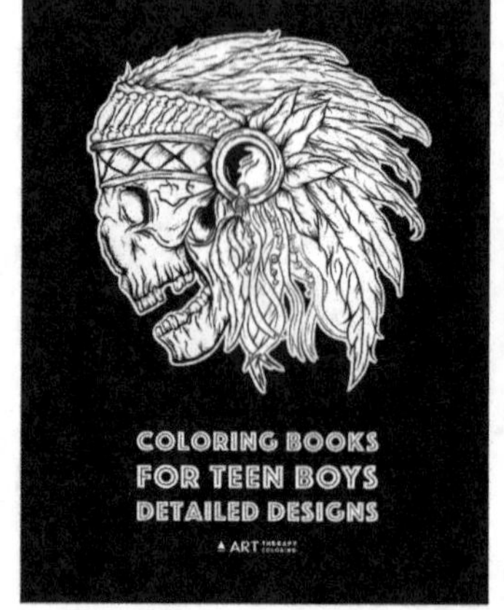
COLORING BOOKS
FOR TEEN BOYS
DETAILED DESIGNS
ART THERAPY COLORING

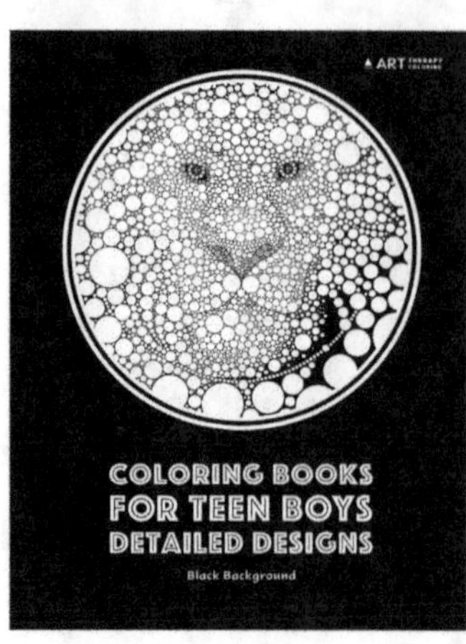
ART THERAPY COLORING
COLORING BOOKS
FOR TEEN BOYS
DETAILED DESIGNS
Black Background

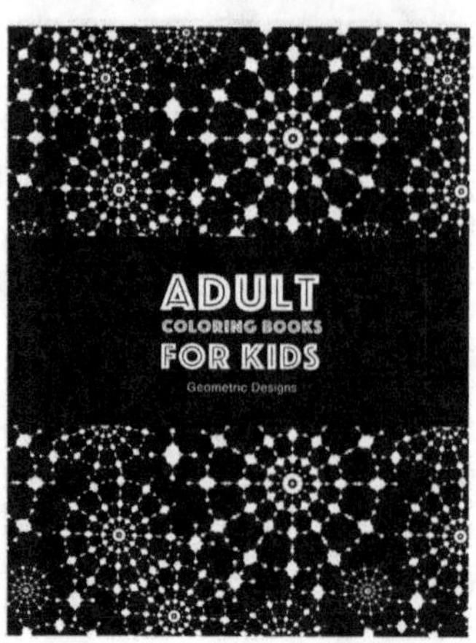
ADULT
COLORING BOOKS
FOR KIDS
Geometric Designs

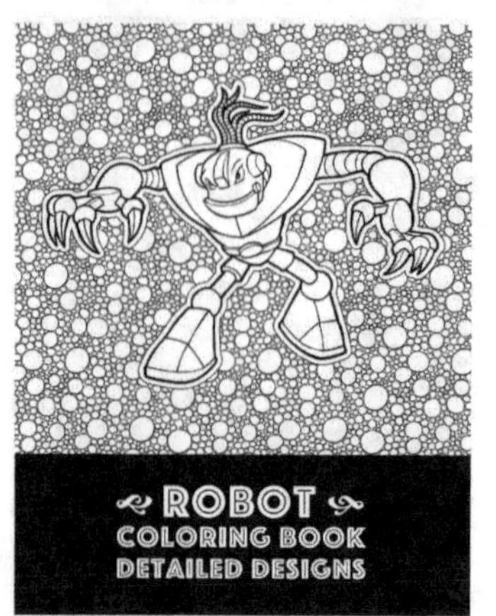
ROBOT
COLORING BOOK
DETAILED DESIGNS

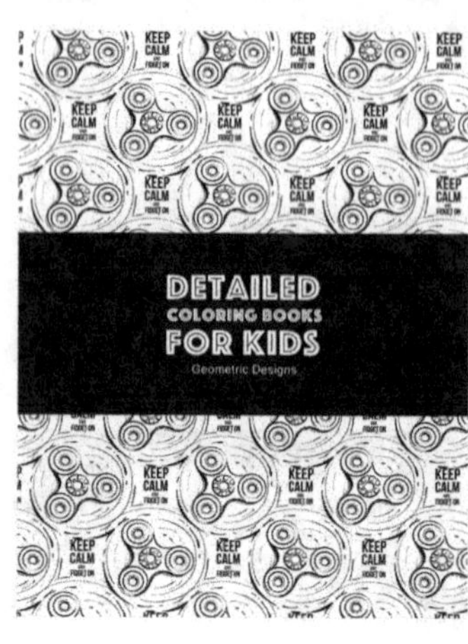
KEEP CALM
DETAILED
COLORING BOOKS
FOR KIDS
Geometric Designs

Art Therapy Coloring Books

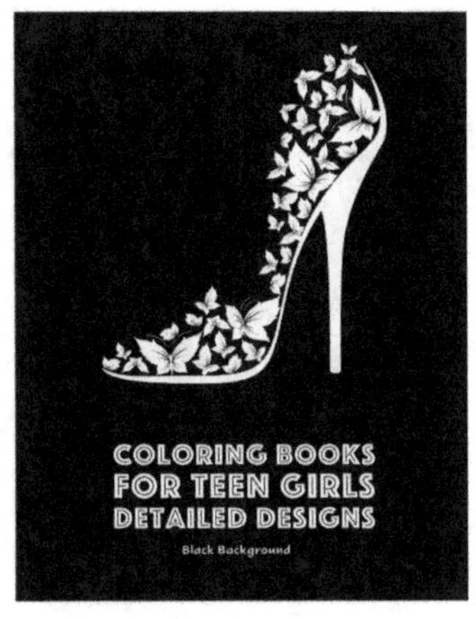

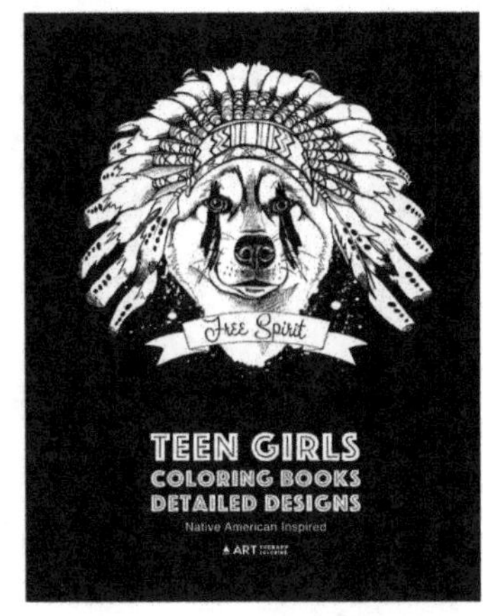

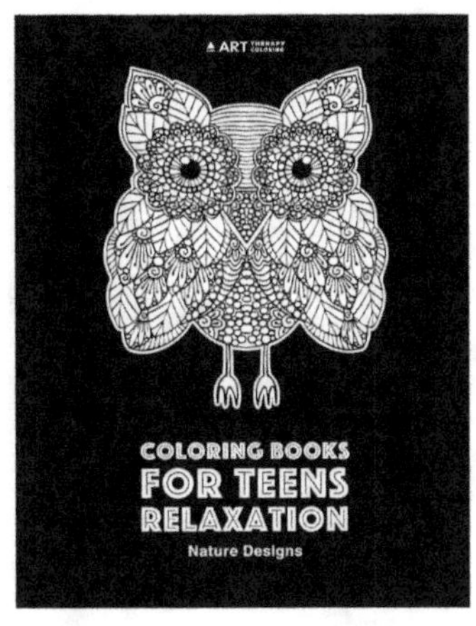

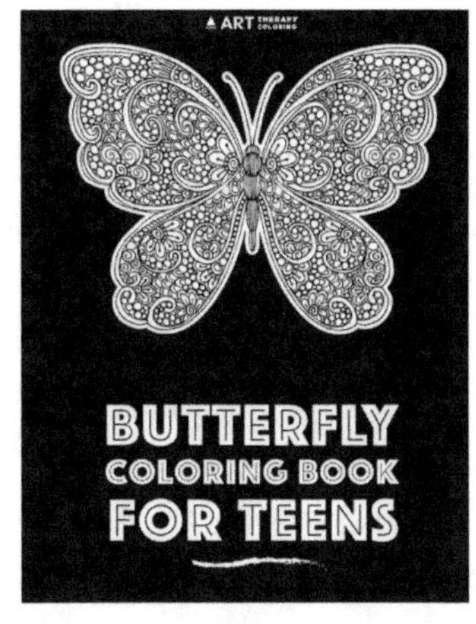

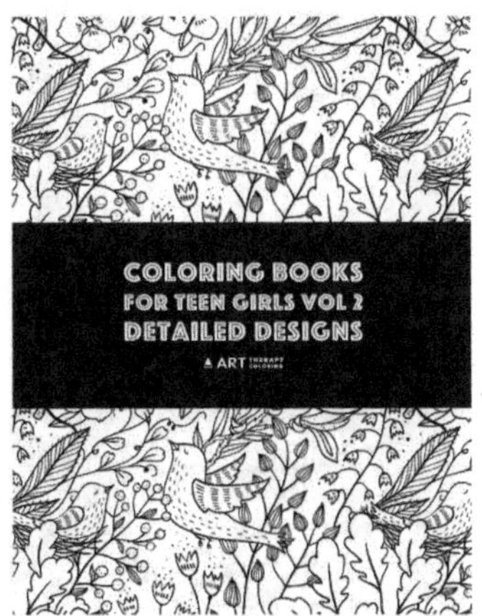

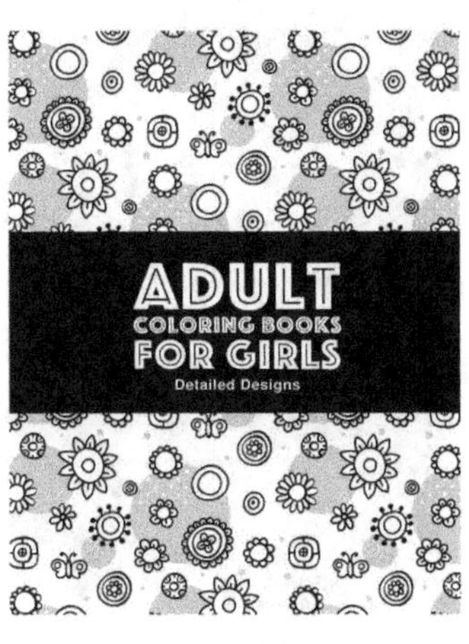

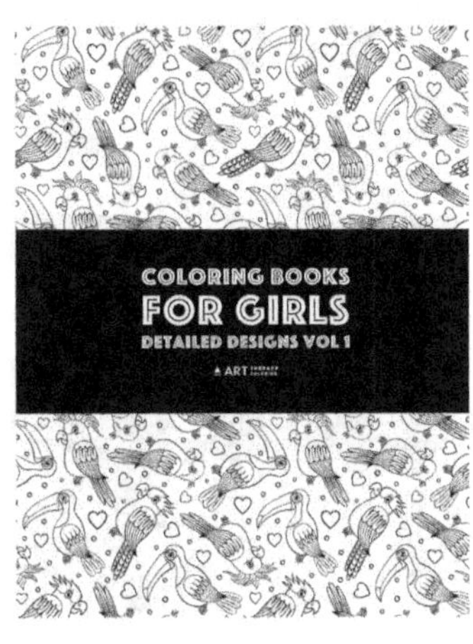

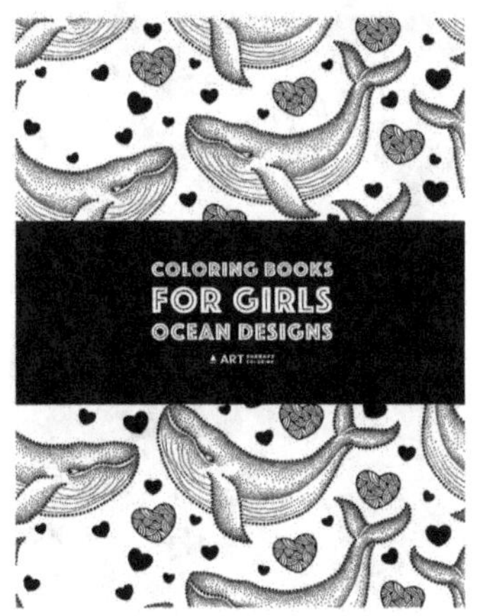

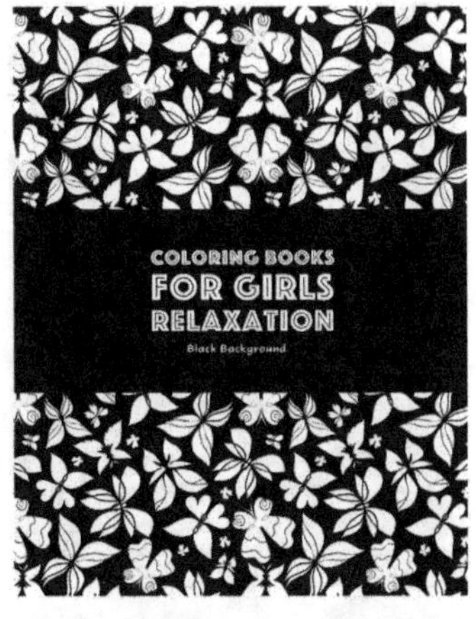

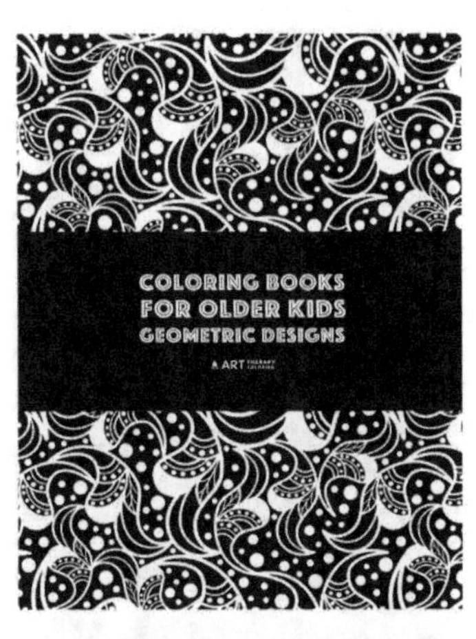

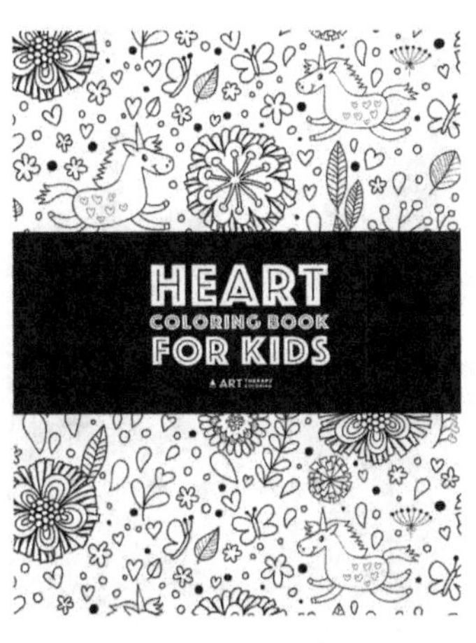

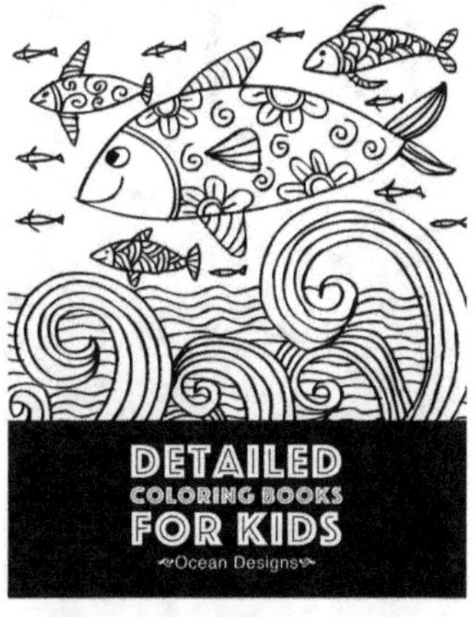

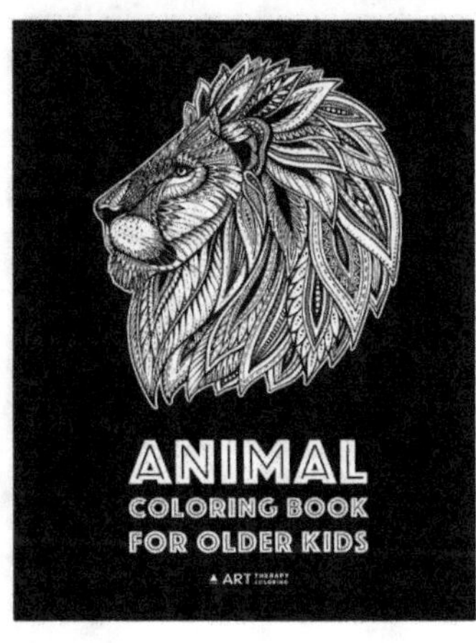

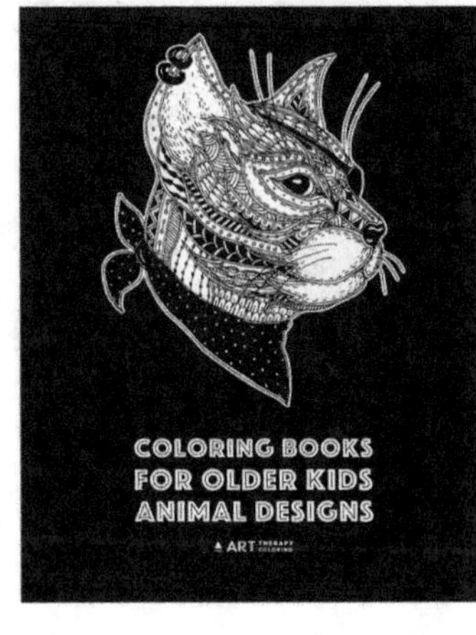

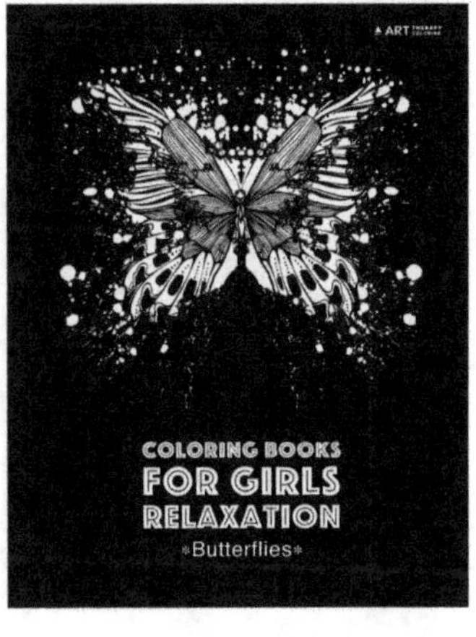

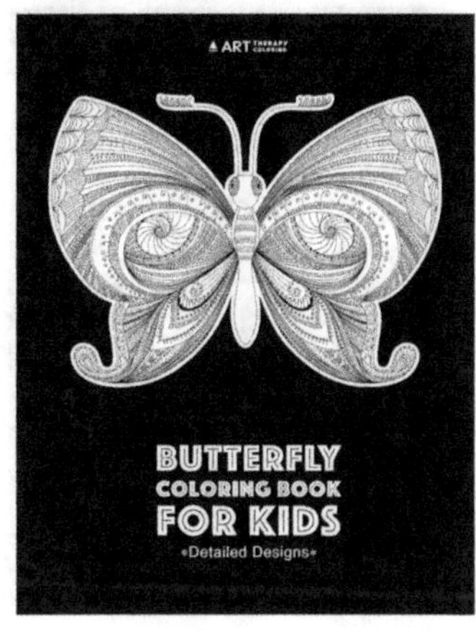

Coloring Books For Kids

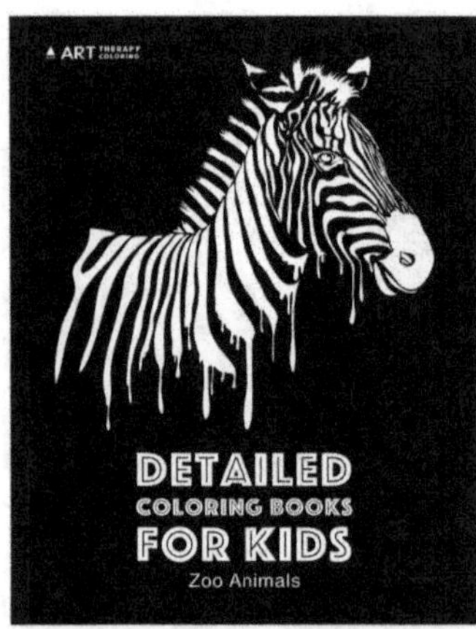

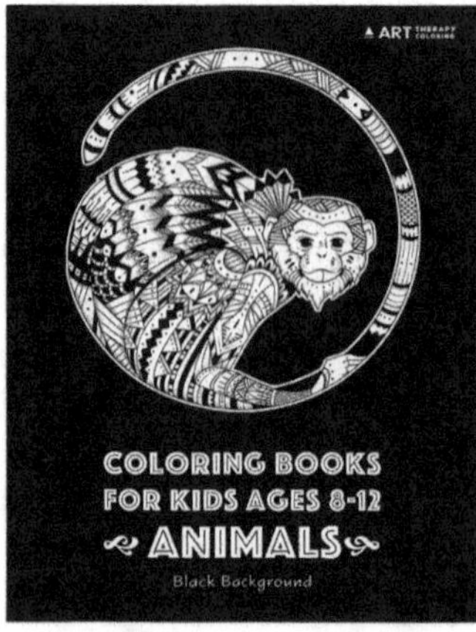

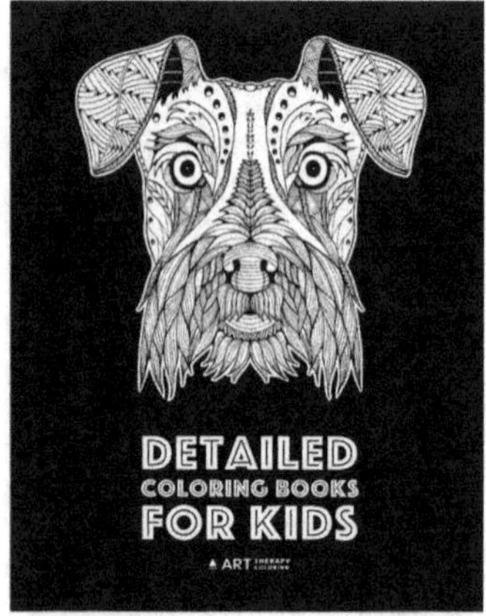

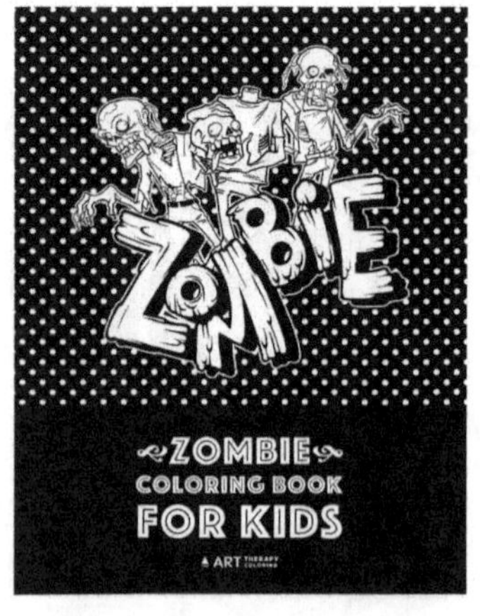

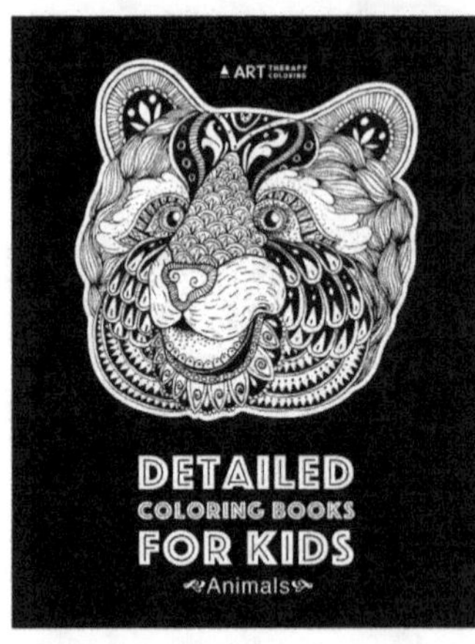

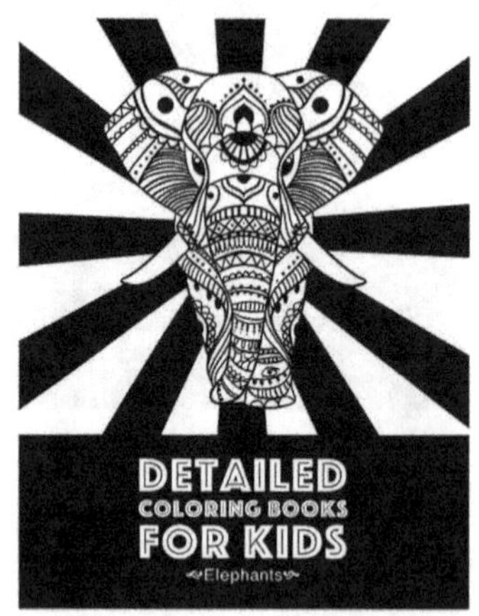

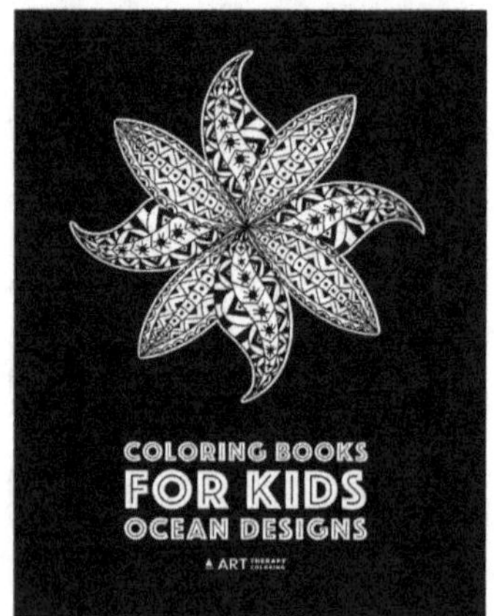

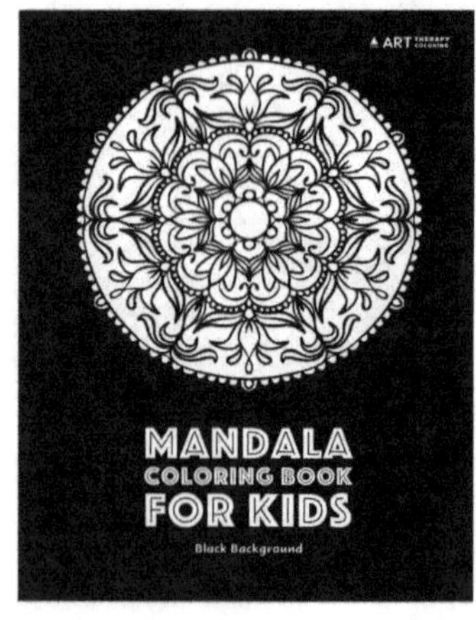

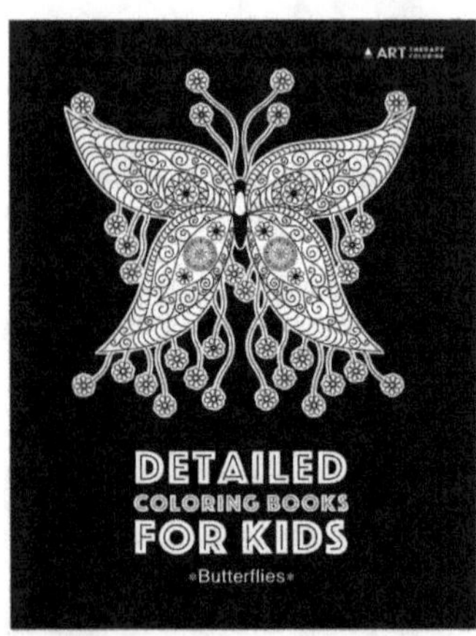

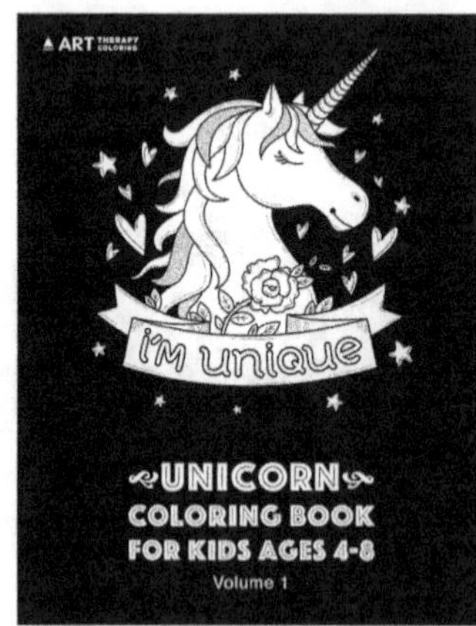

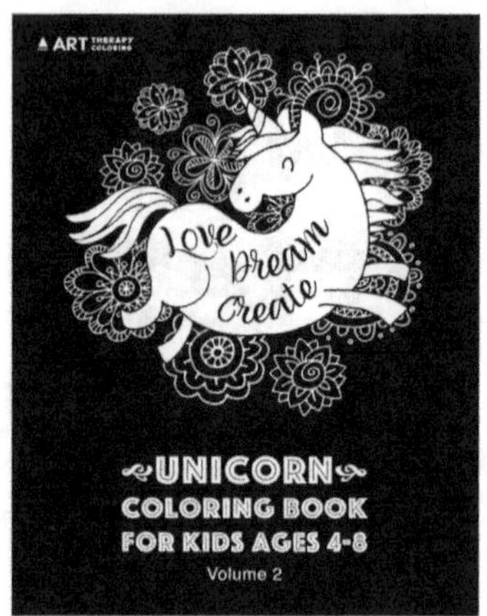

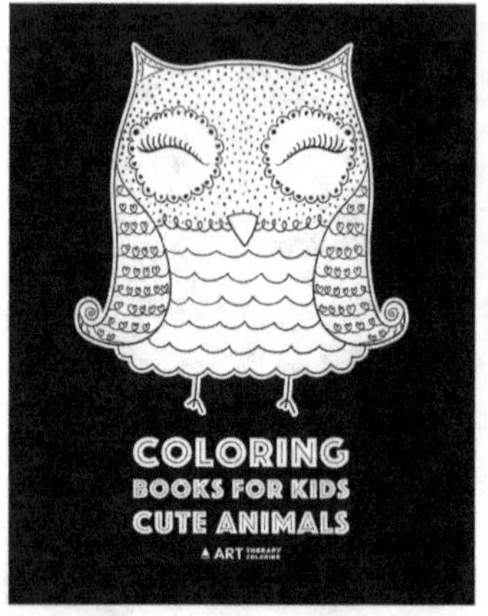

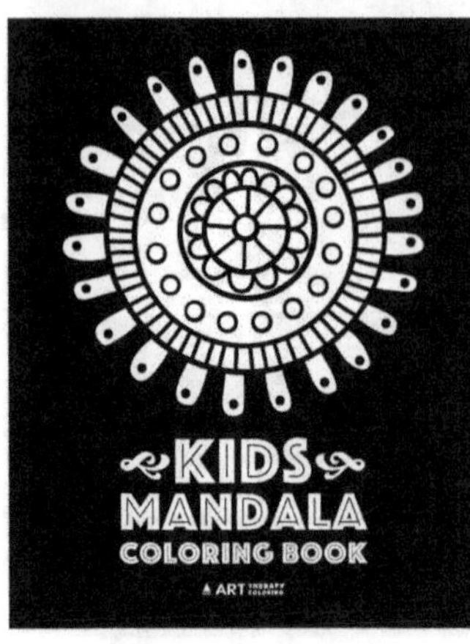

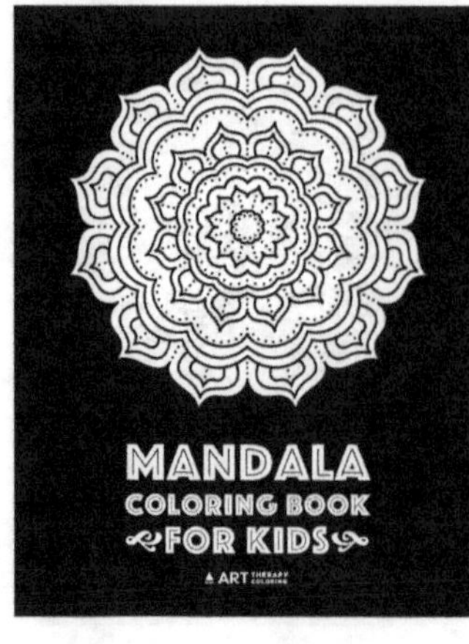

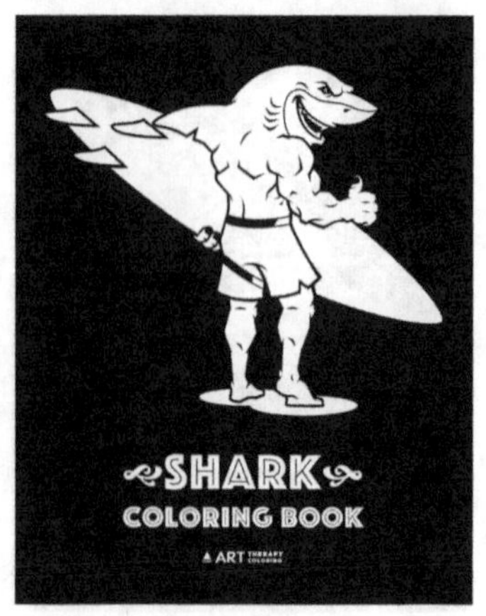

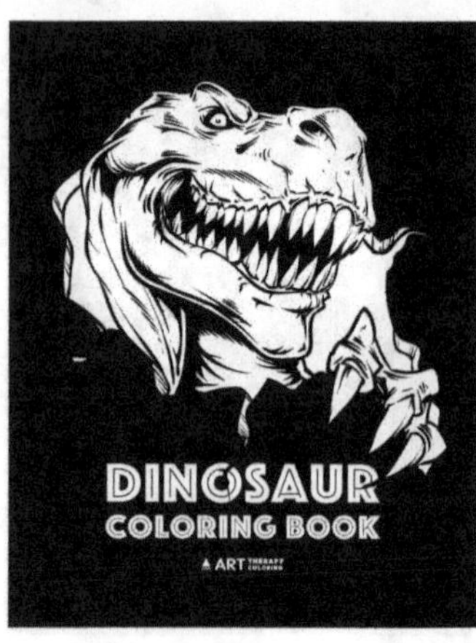

Coloring Books For Adults

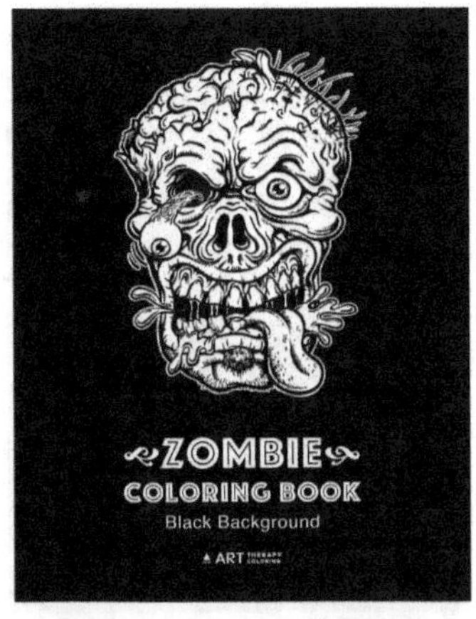

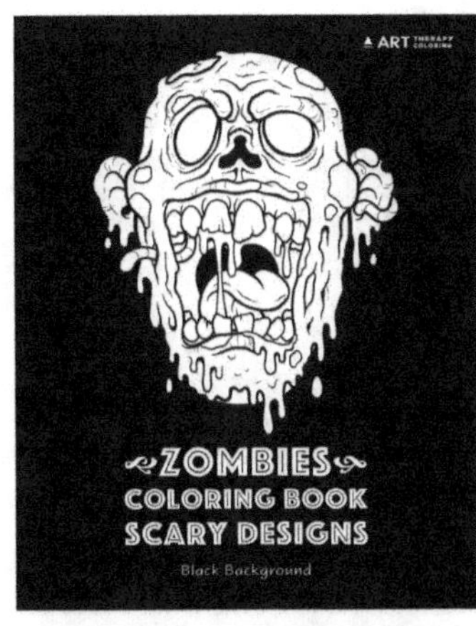

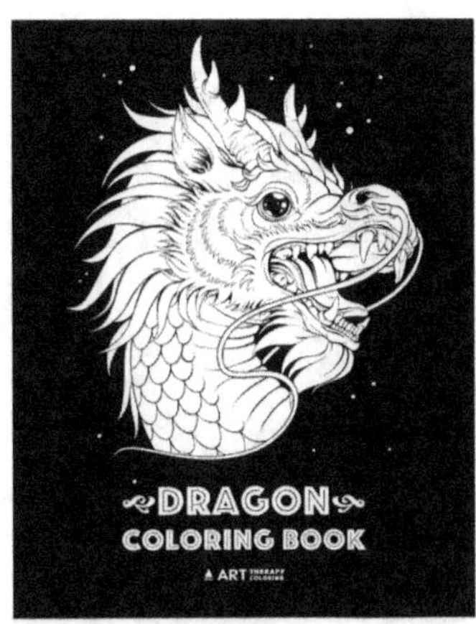

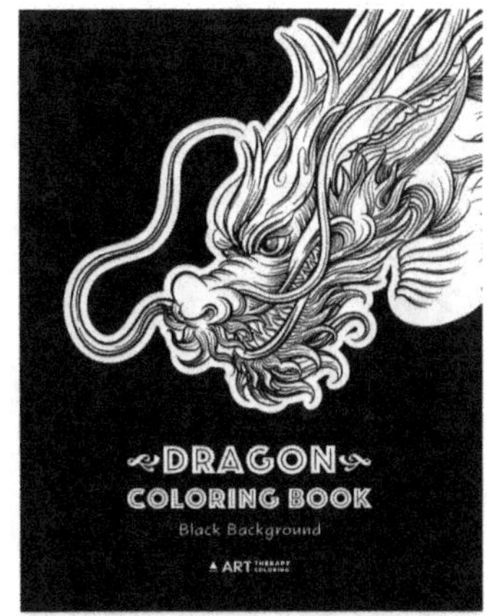

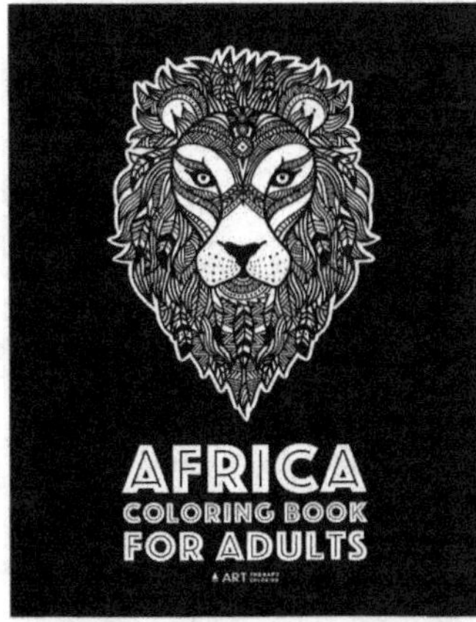

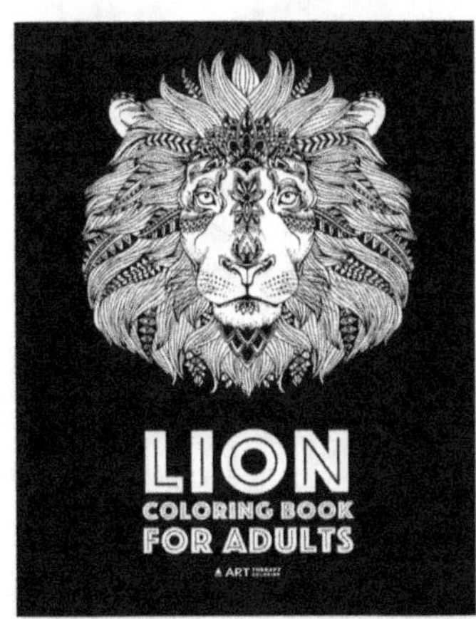

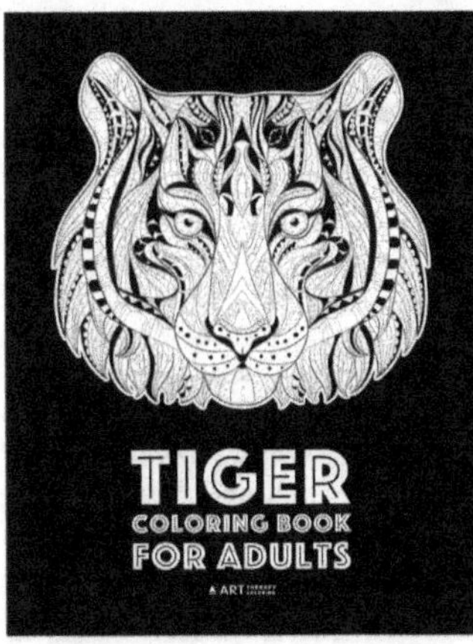

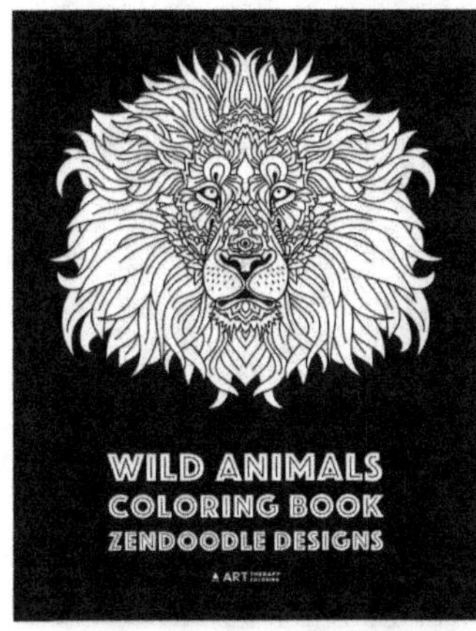

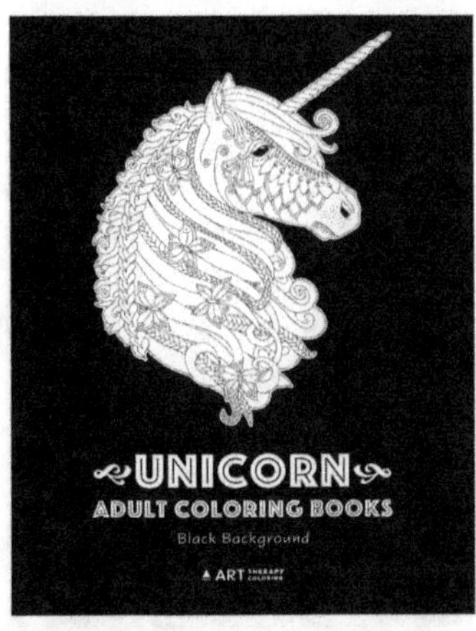

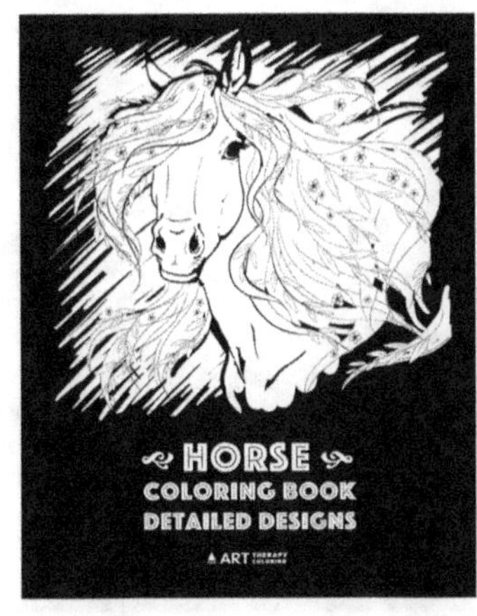

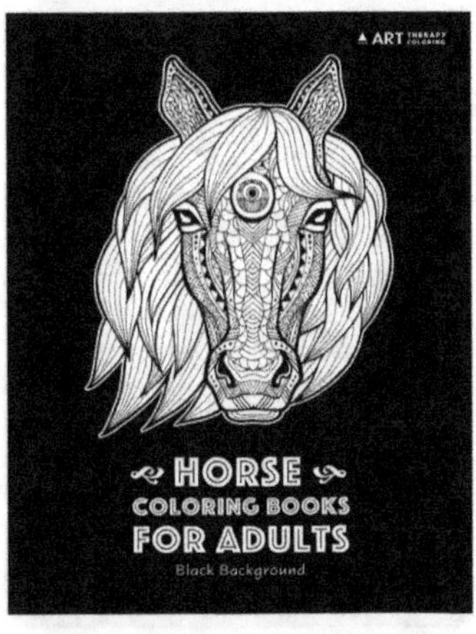

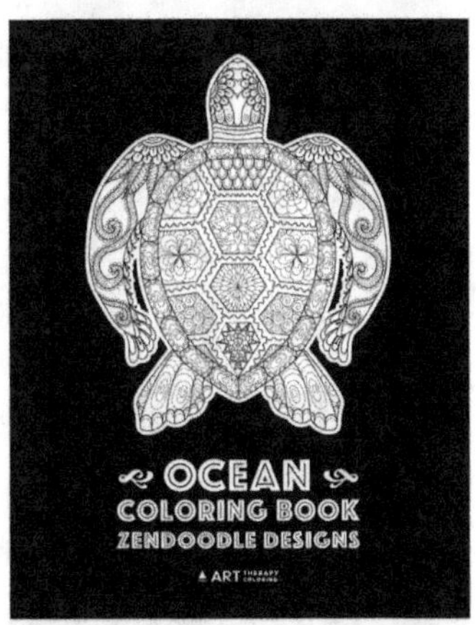

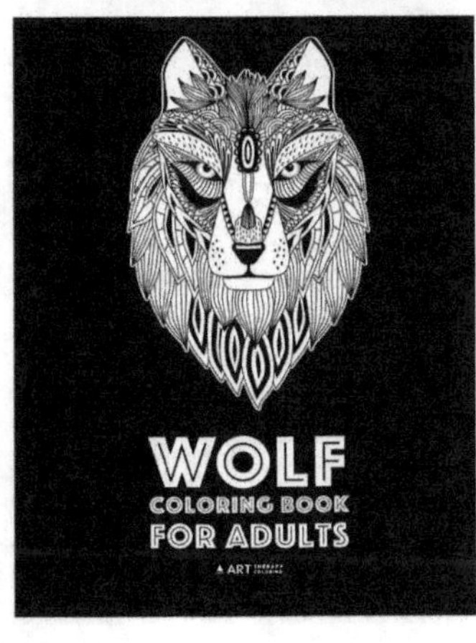

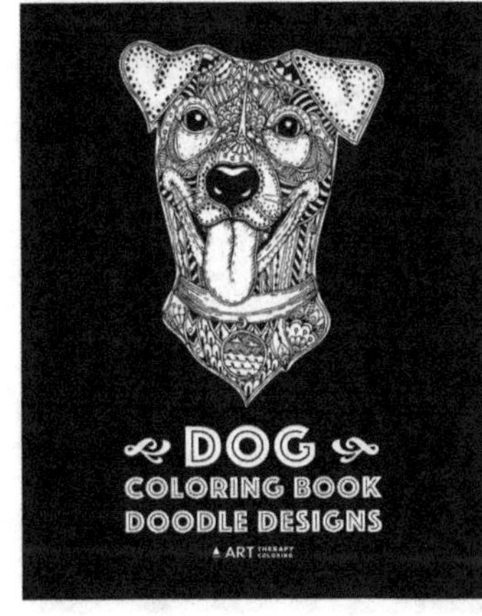

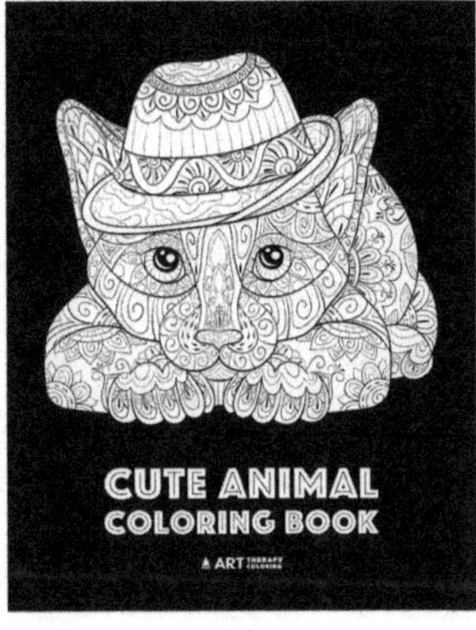

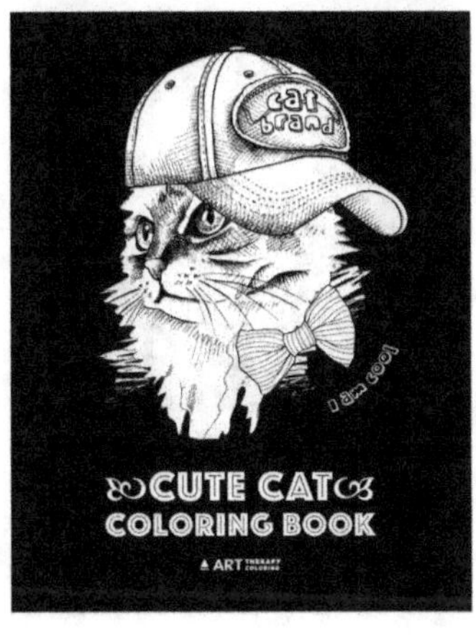

Coloring Books For Adults

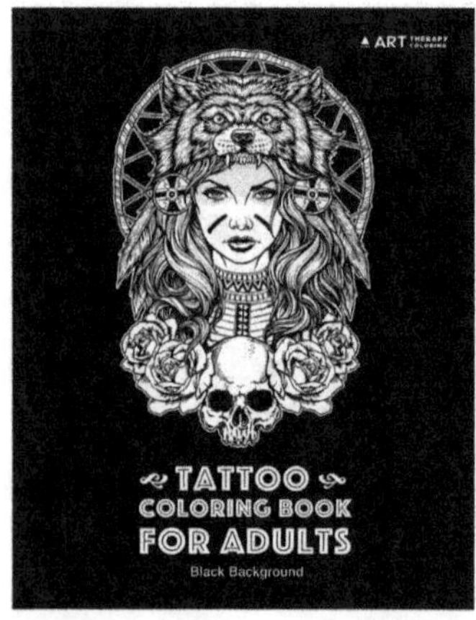

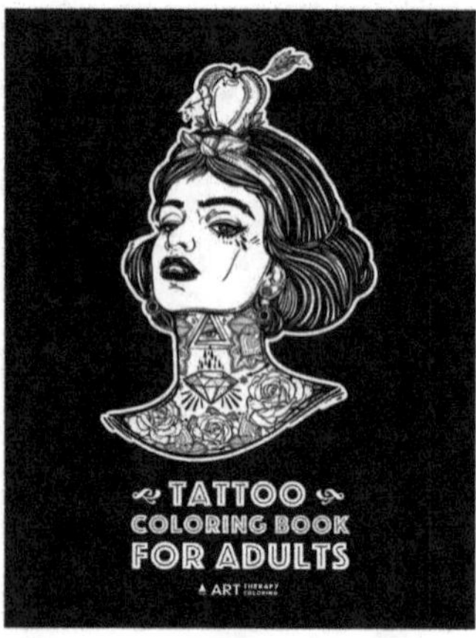

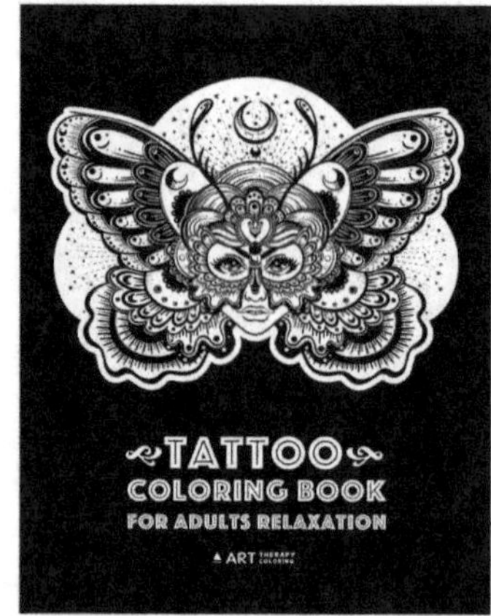

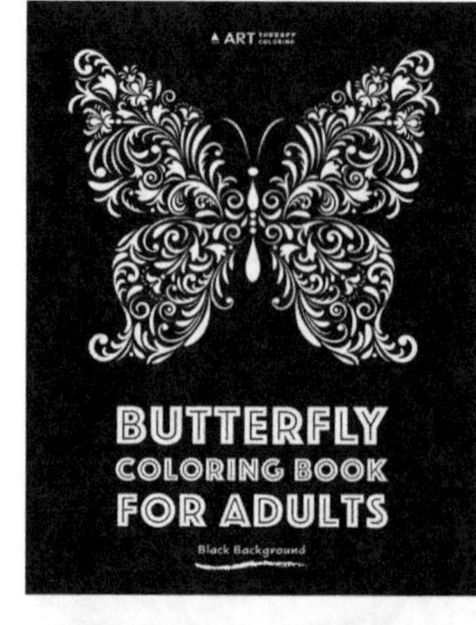

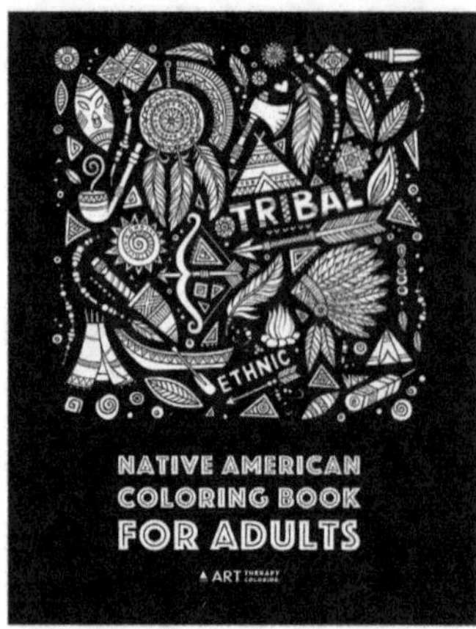

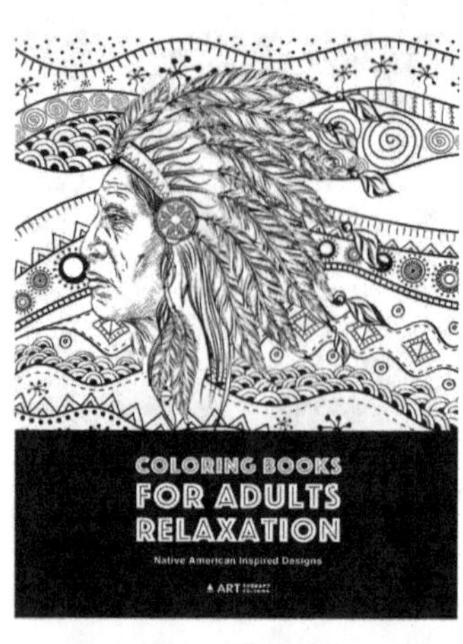

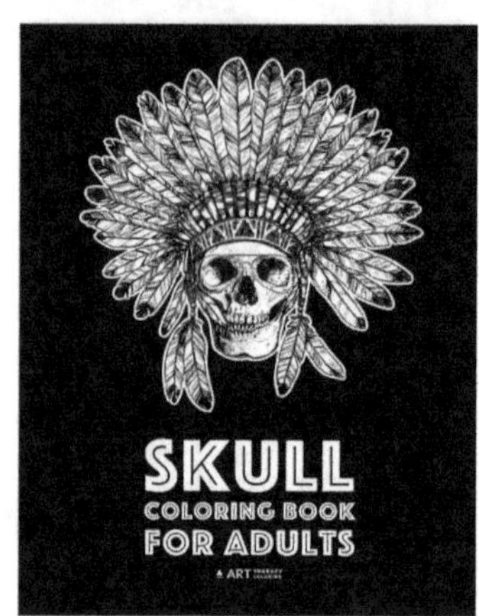

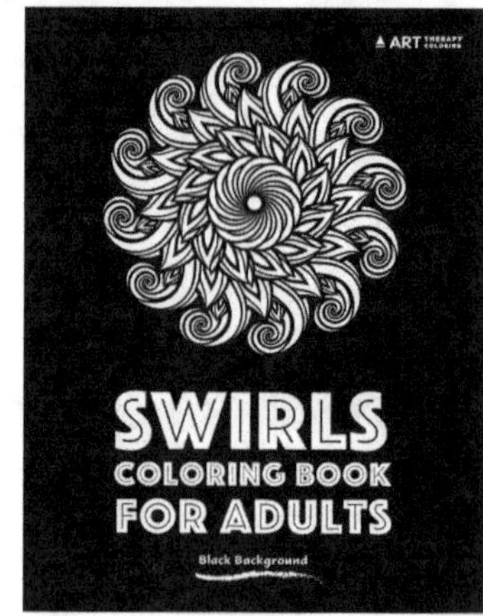

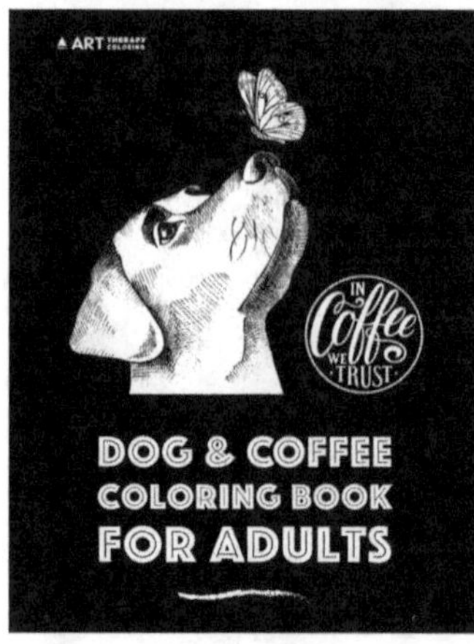

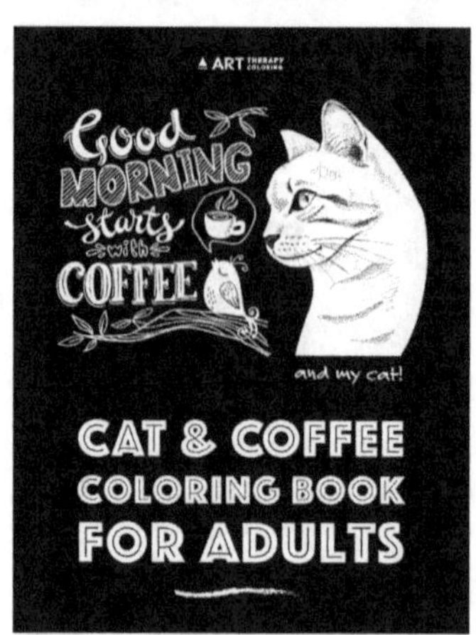

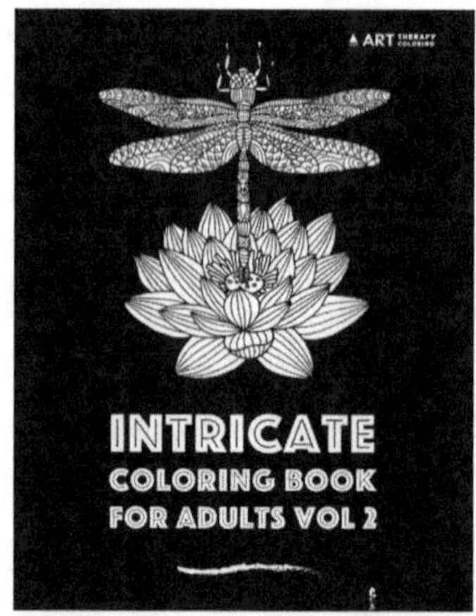

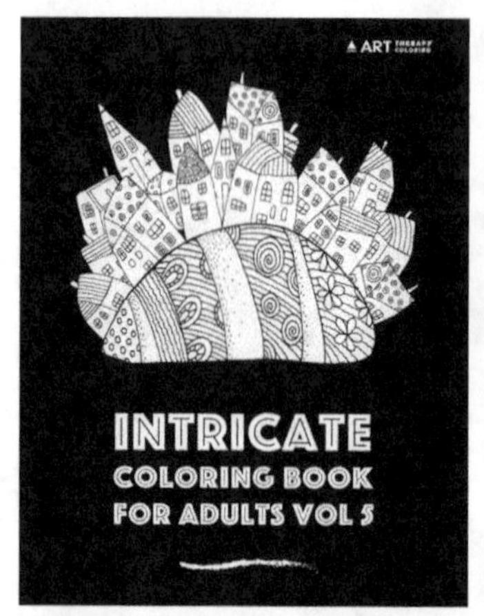

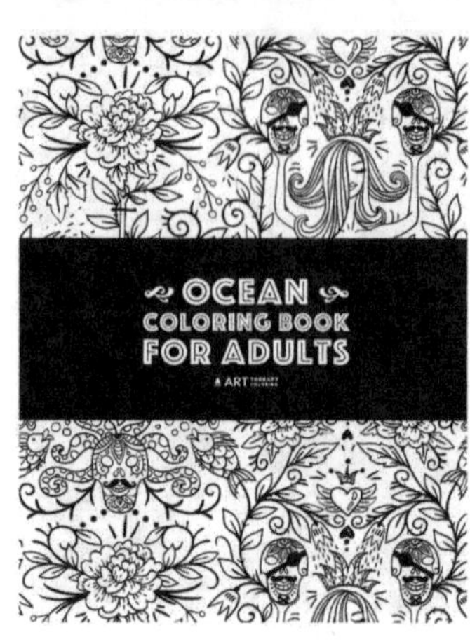

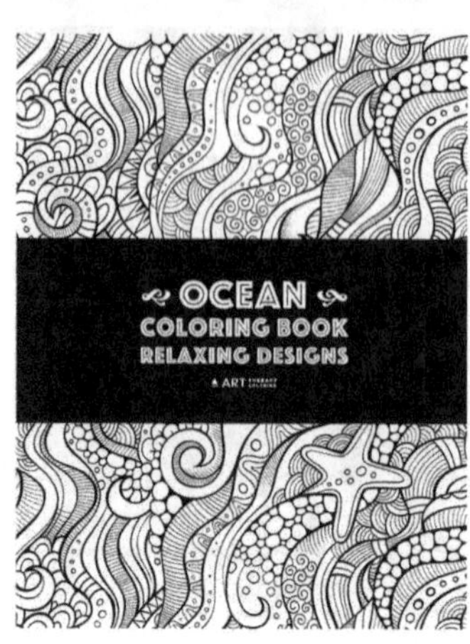

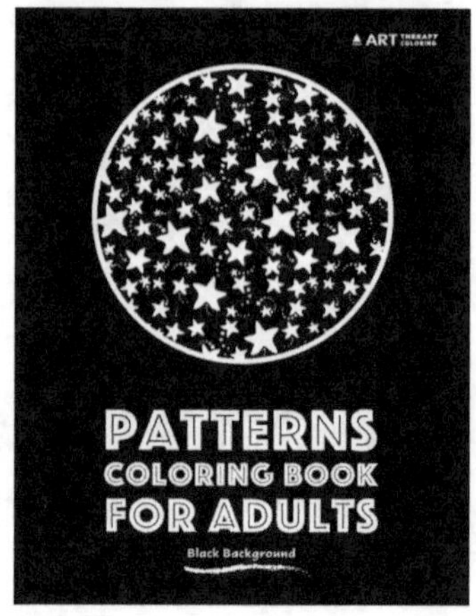

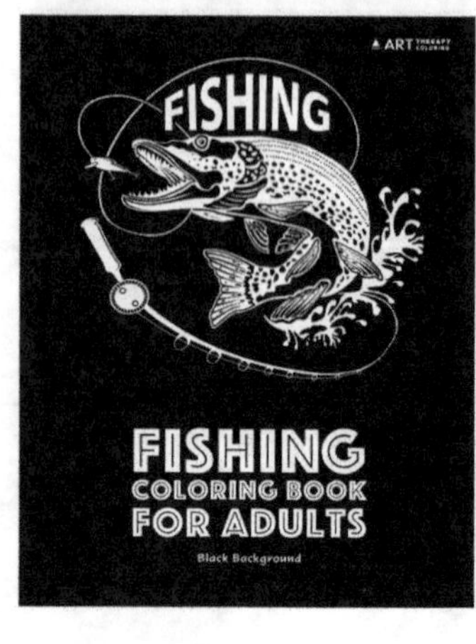

Coloring Books For Adults

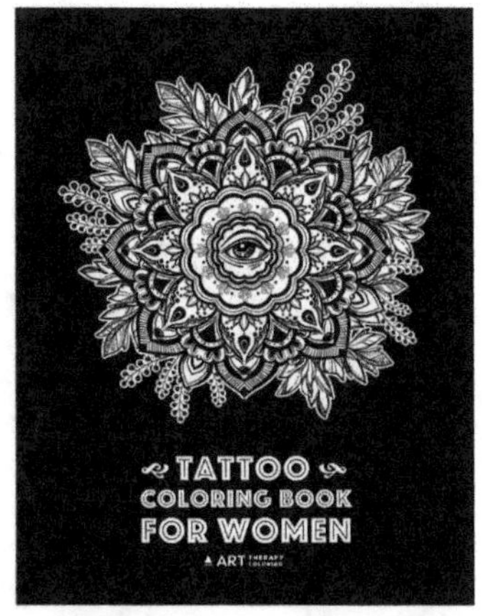
TATTOO
COLORING BOOK
FOR WOMEN

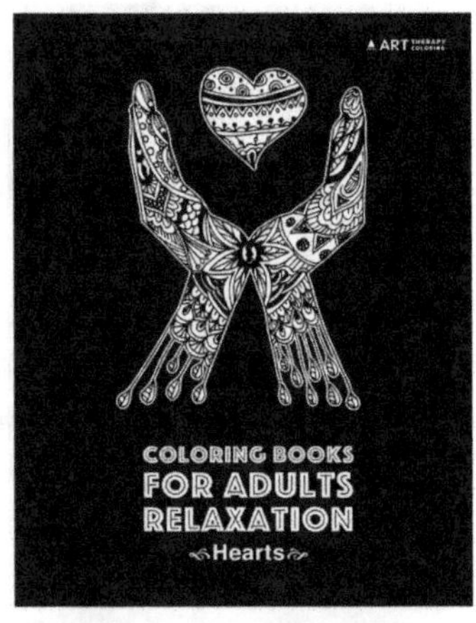
COLORING BOOKS
FOR ADULTS
RELAXATION
Hearts

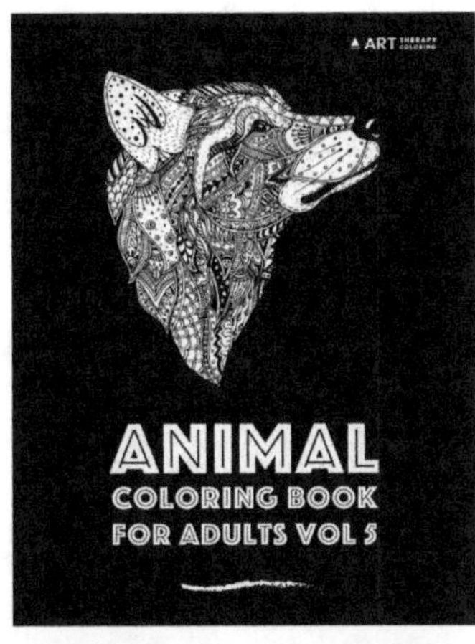
ANIMAL
COLORING BOOK
FOR ADULTS VOL 5

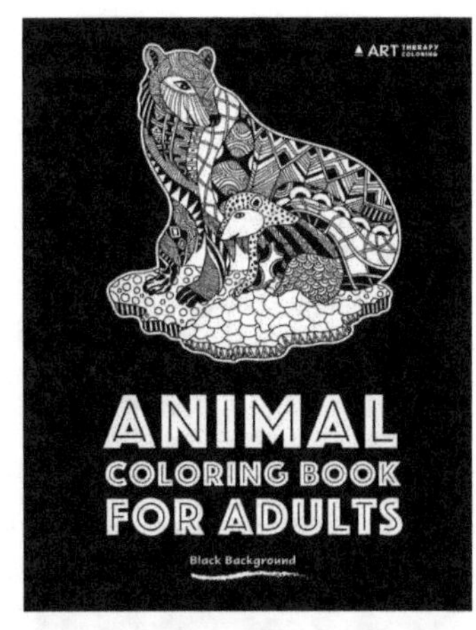
ANIMAL
COLORING BOOK
FOR ADULTS
Black Background

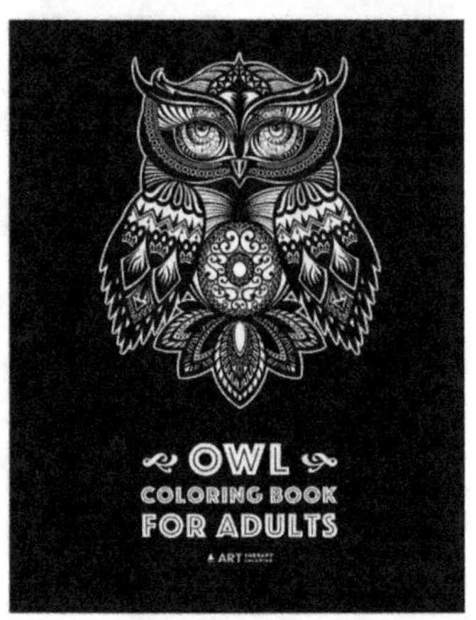
OWL
COLORING BOOK
FOR ADULTS

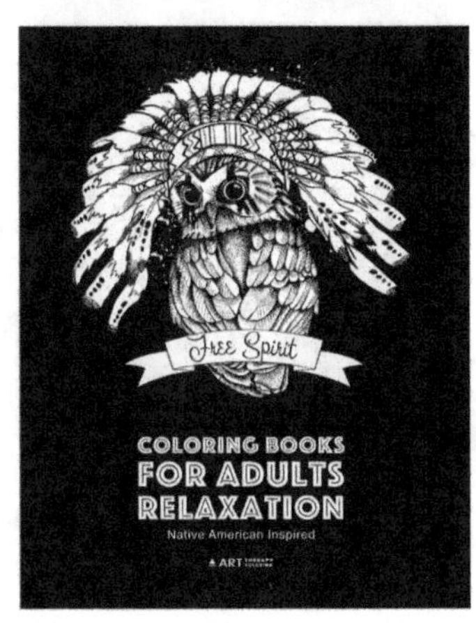
Free Spirit
COLORING BOOKS
FOR ADULTS
RELAXATION
Native American Inspired

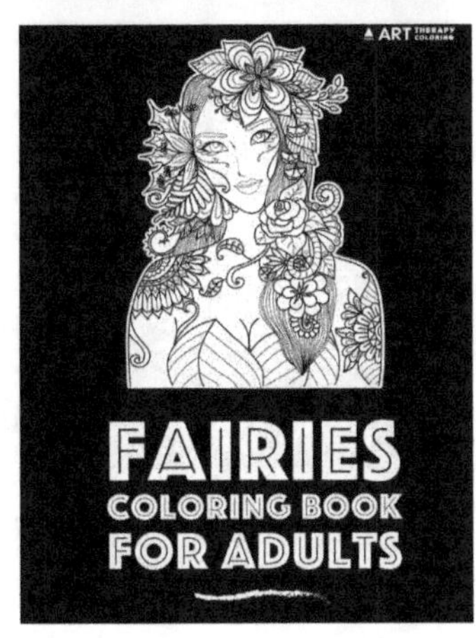
FAIRIES
COLORING BOOK
FOR ADULTS

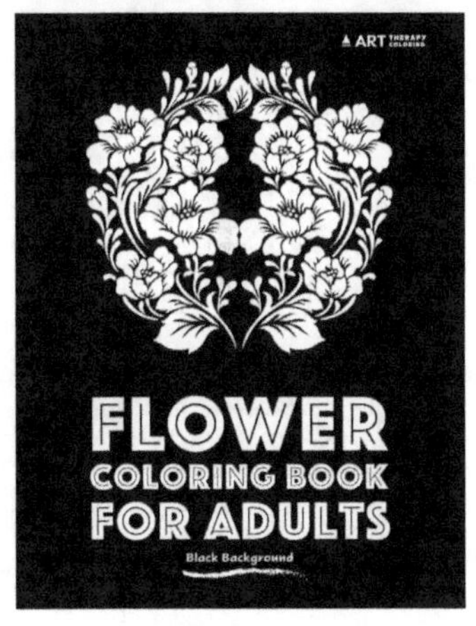
FLOWER
COLORING BOOK
FOR ADULTS
Black Background

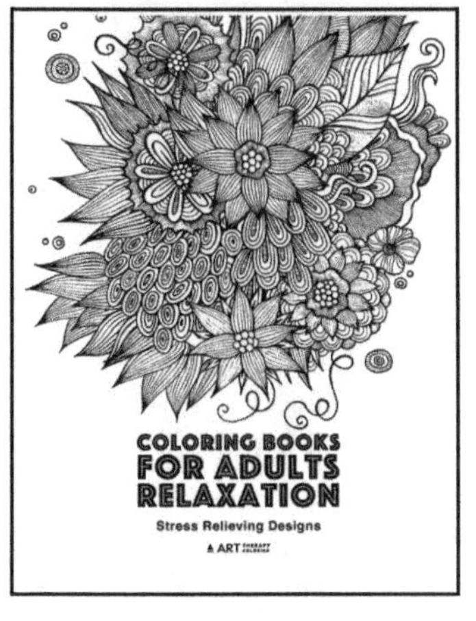
COLORING BOOKS
FOR ADULTS
RELAXATION
Stress Relieving Designs

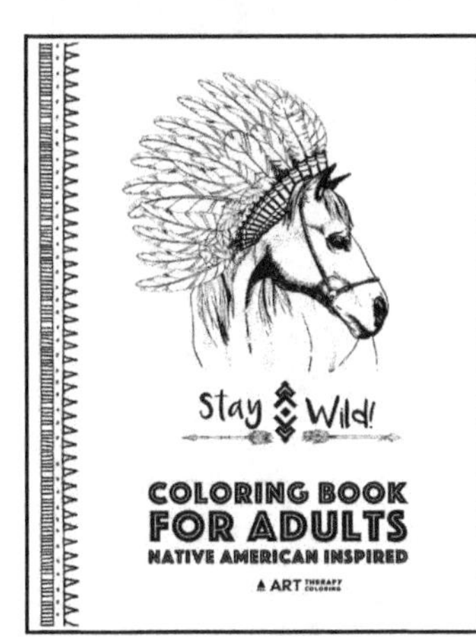
Stay Wild!
COLORING BOOK
FOR ADULTS
NATIVE AMERICAN INSPIRED
ART

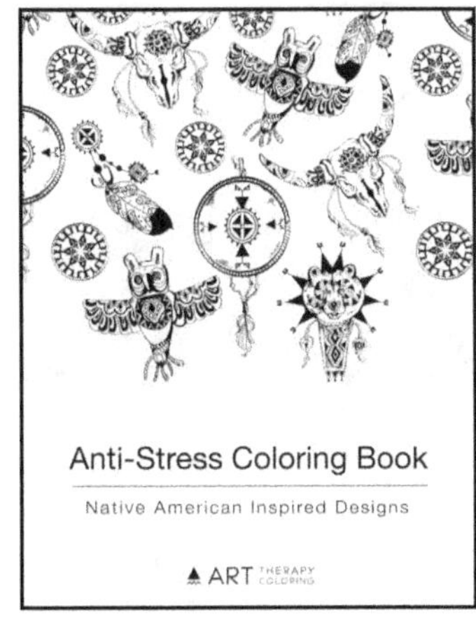
Anti-Stress Coloring Book
Native American Inspired Designs
ART THERAPY COLORING

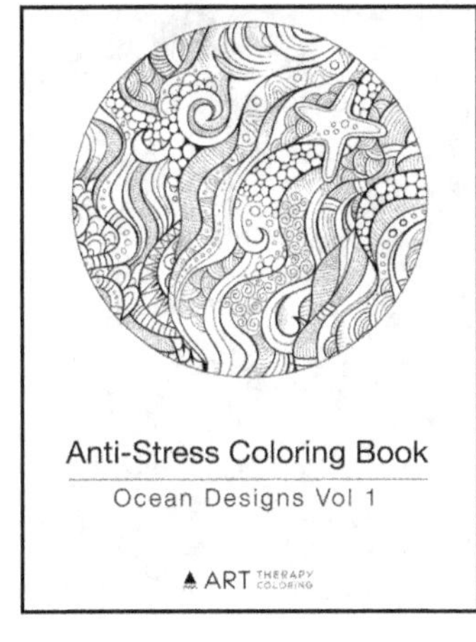
Anti-Stress Coloring Book
Ocean Designs Vol 1
ART THERAPY COLORING

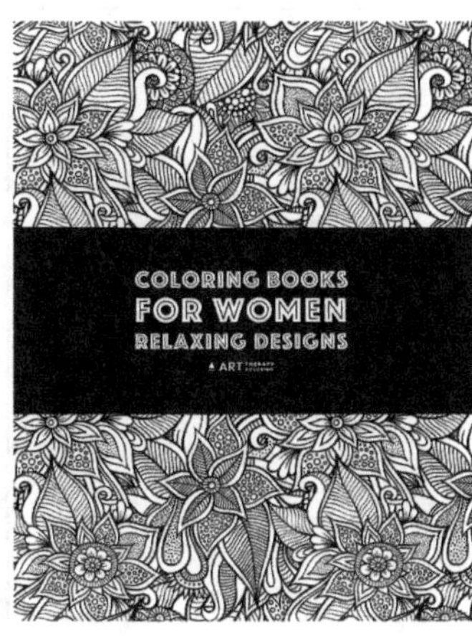
COLORING BOOKS
FOR WOMEN
RELAXING DESIGNS

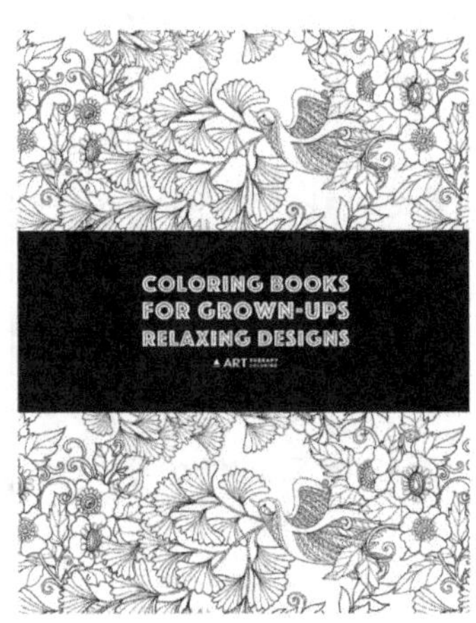
COLORING BOOKS
FOR GROWN-UPS
RELAXING DESIGNS

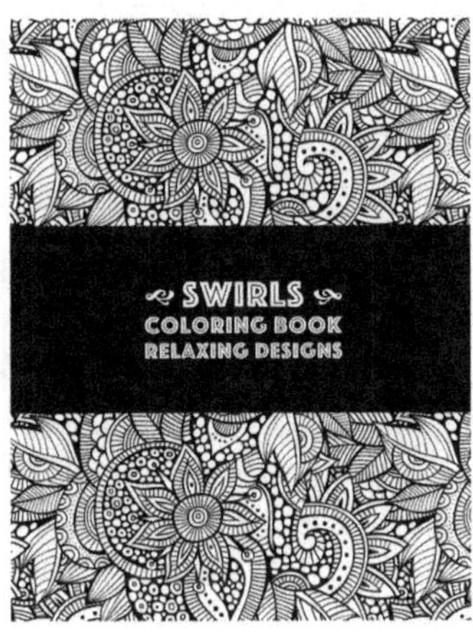
SWIRLS
COLORING BOOK
RELAXING DESIGNS

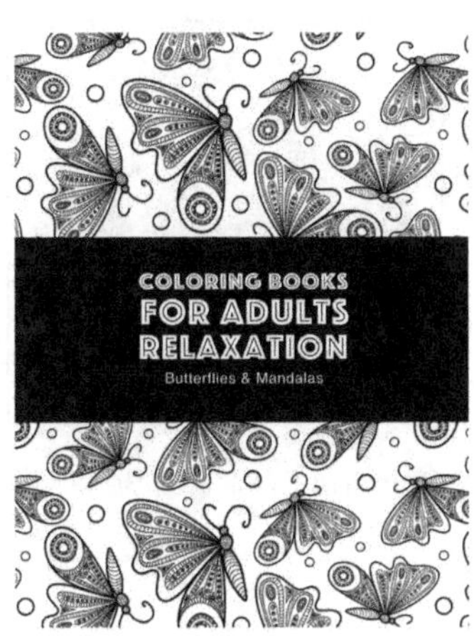
COLORING BOOKS
FOR ADULTS
RELAXATION
Butterflies & Mandalas

Coloring Books For Seniors

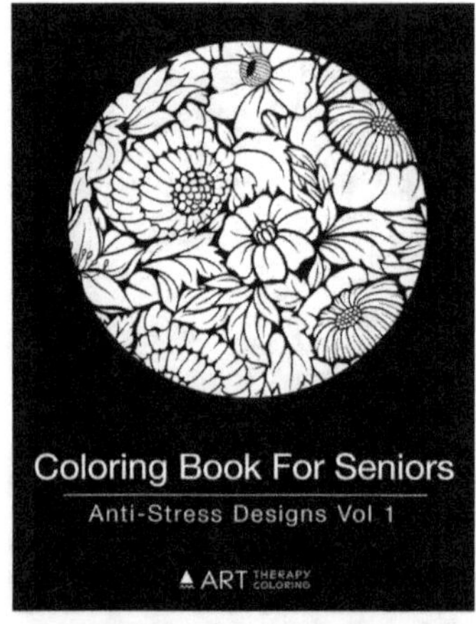

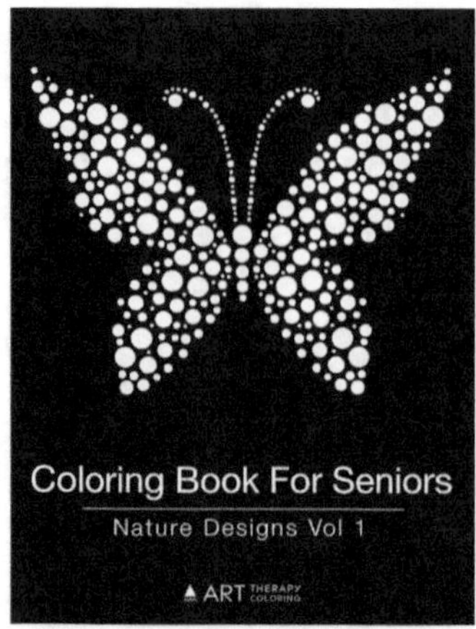

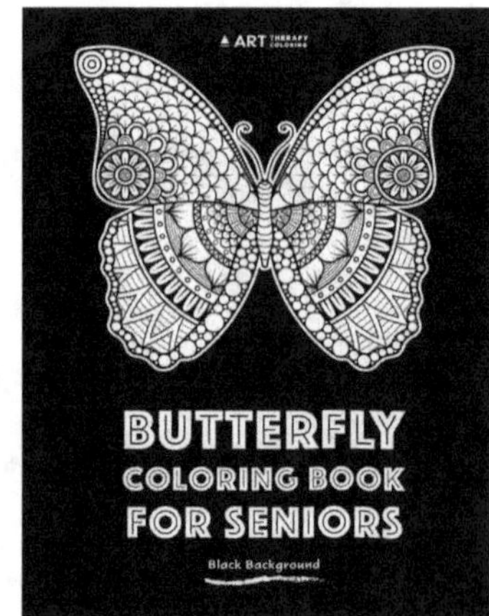

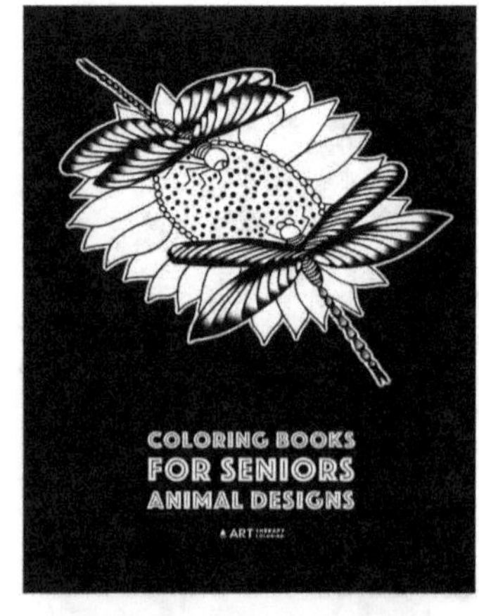

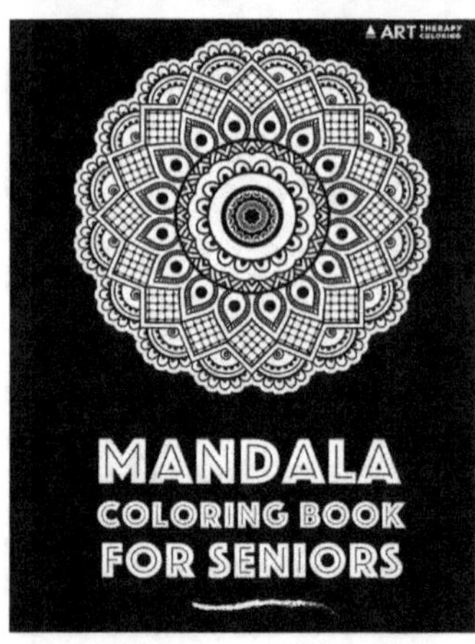

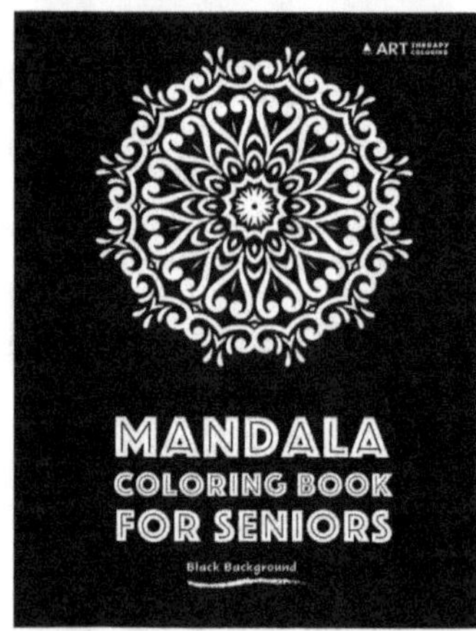

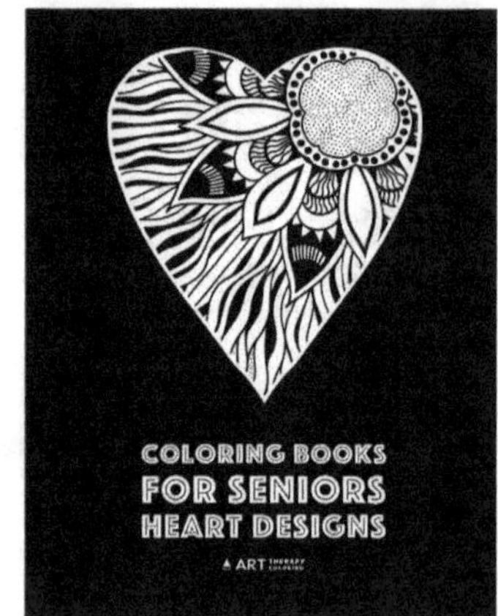

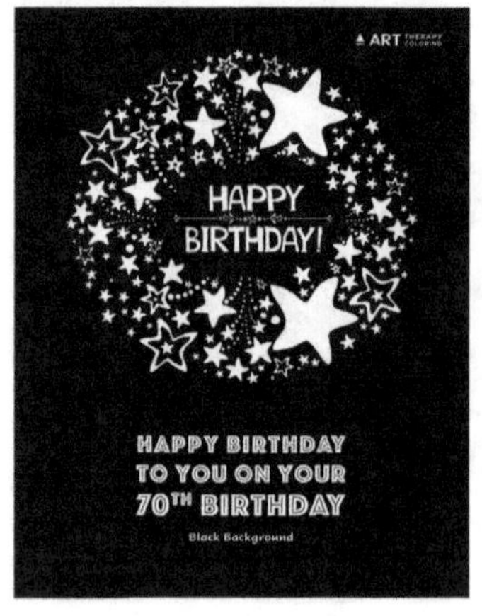

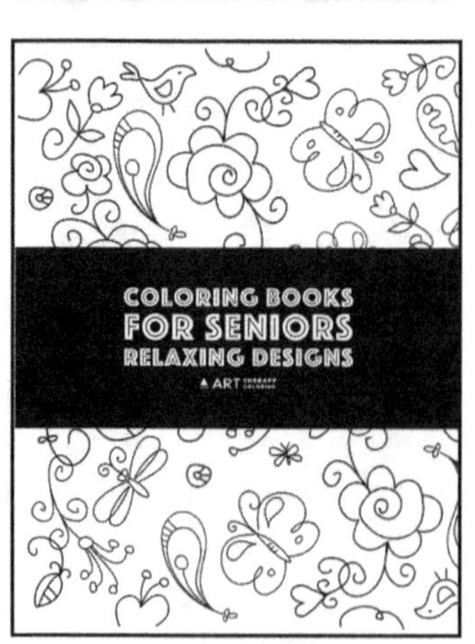

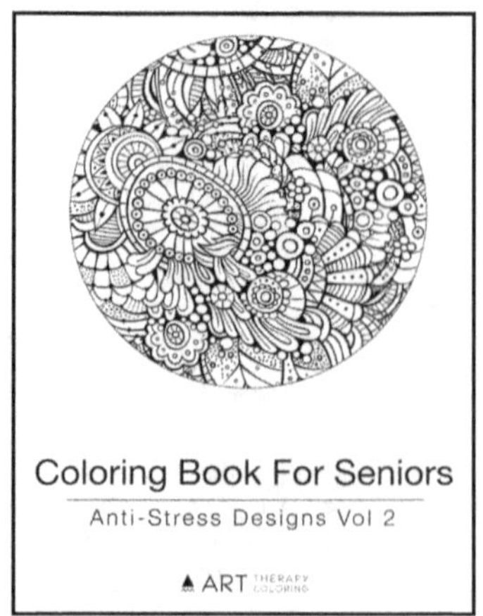

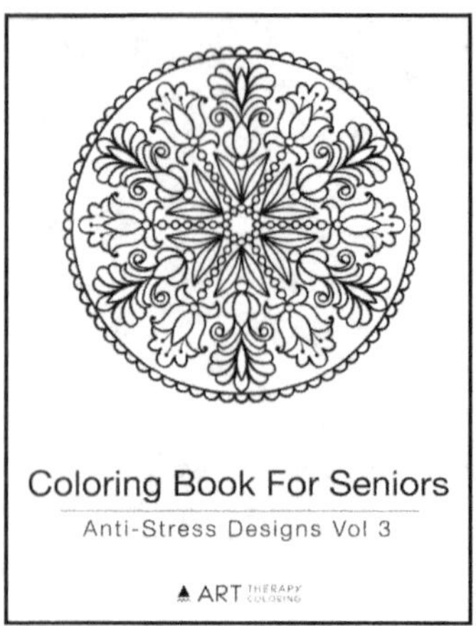

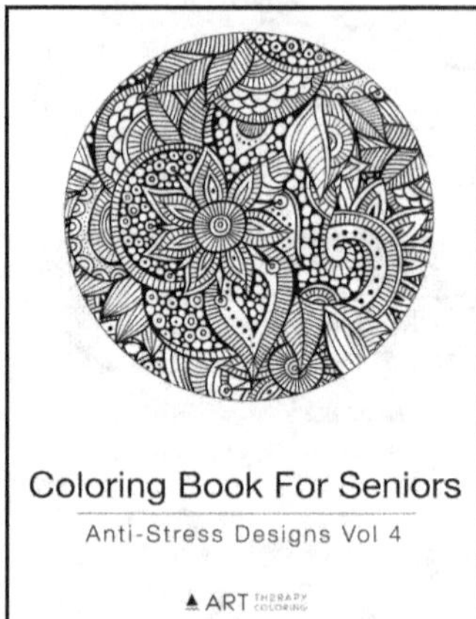

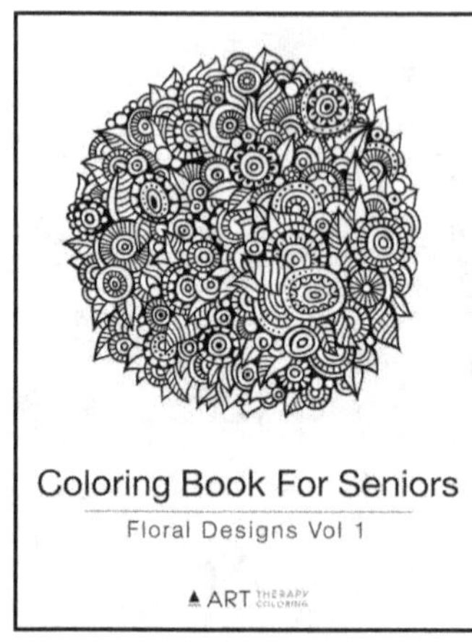

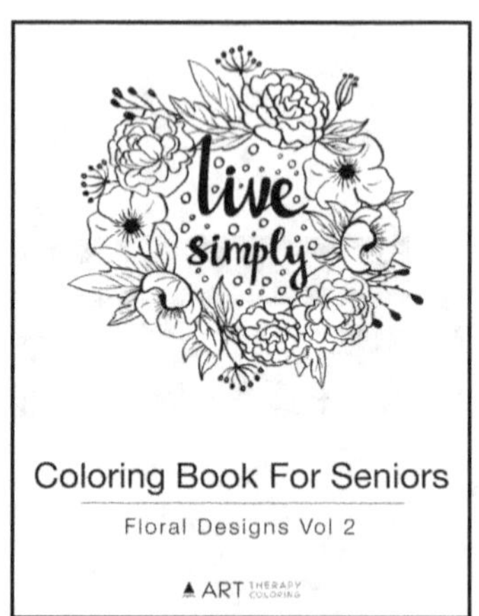

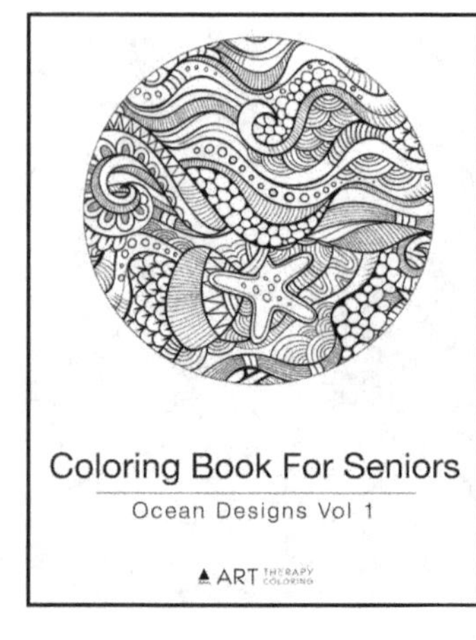

Coloring Books For Men

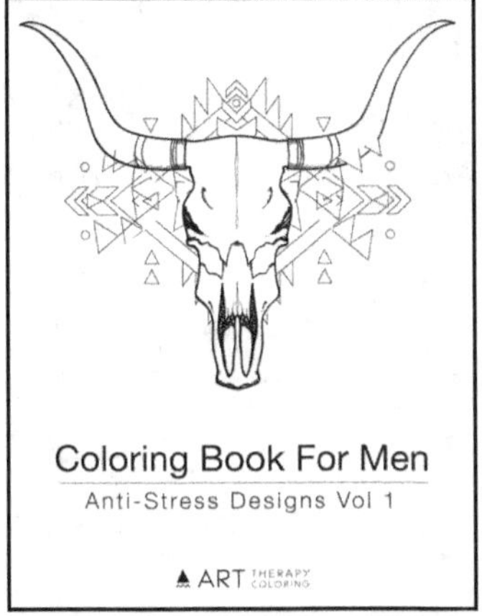
Coloring Book For Men
Anti-Stress Designs Vol 1
ART THERAPY COLORING

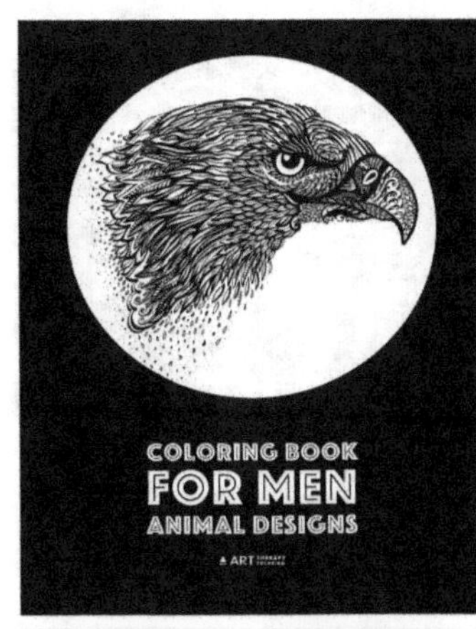
COLORING BOOK
FOR MEN
ANIMAL DESIGNS

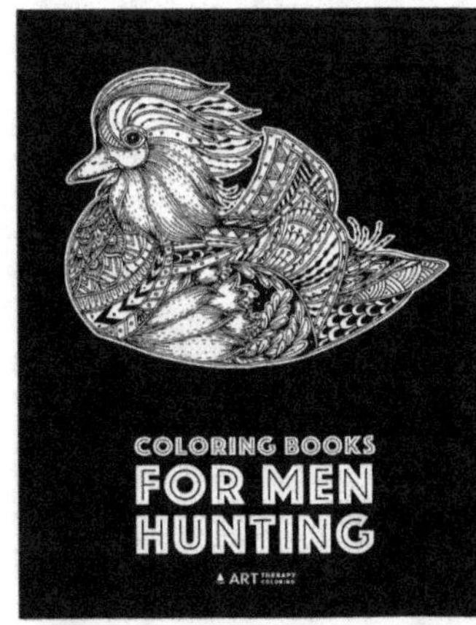
COLORING BOOKS
FOR MEN
HUNTING

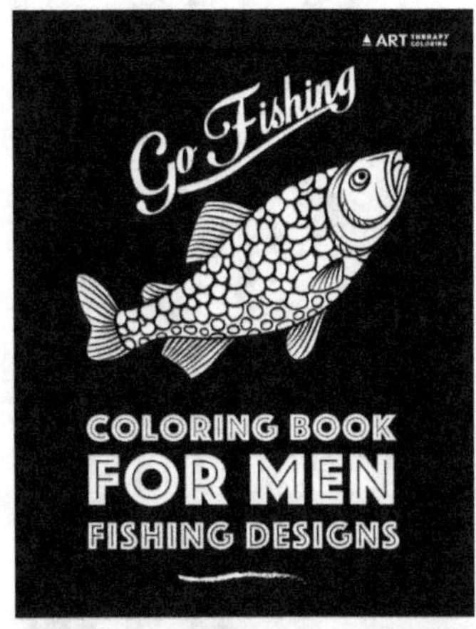
Go Fishing
COLORING BOOK
FOR MEN
FISHING DESIGNS

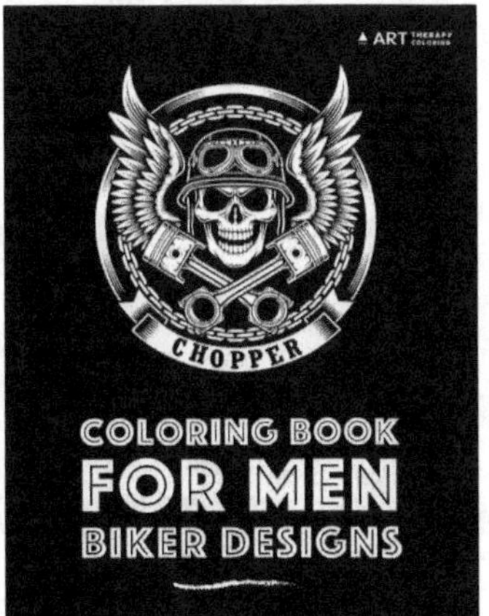
CHOPPER
COLORING BOOK
FOR MEN
BIKER DESIGNS

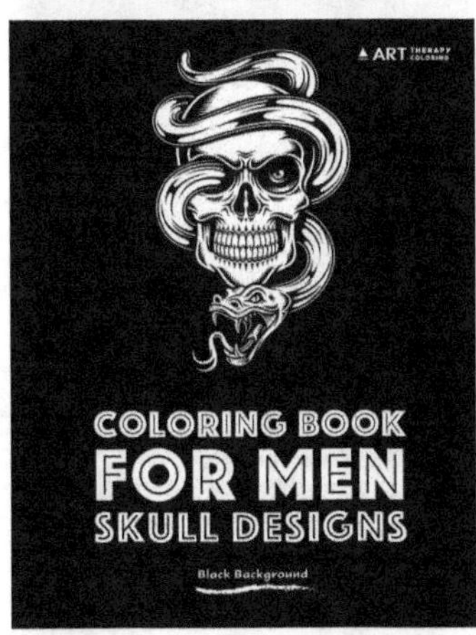
COLORING BOOK
FOR MEN
SKULL DESIGNS
Black Background

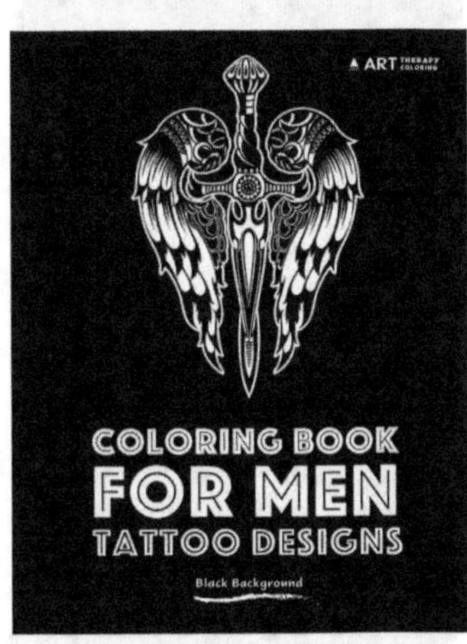
COLORING BOOK
FOR MEN
TATTOO DESIGNS
Black Background

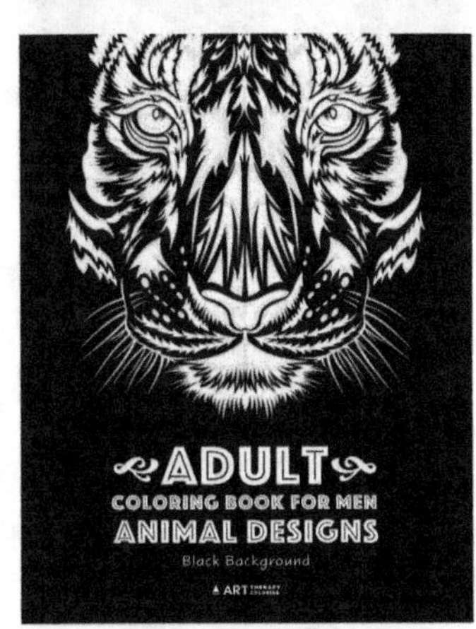
ADULT
COLORING BOOK FOR MEN
ANIMAL DESIGNS
Black Background

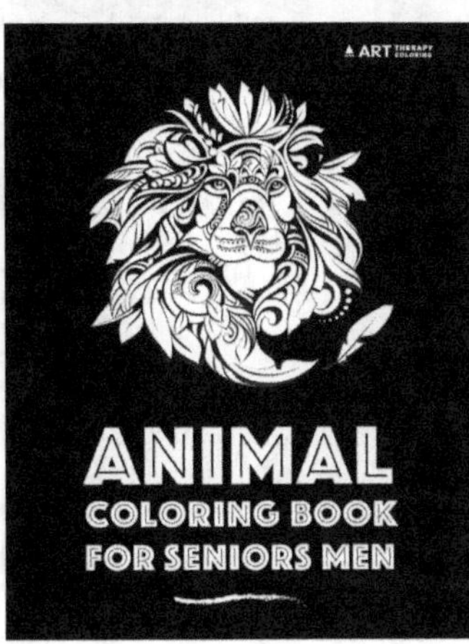
ANIMAL
COLORING BOOK
FOR SENIORS MEN

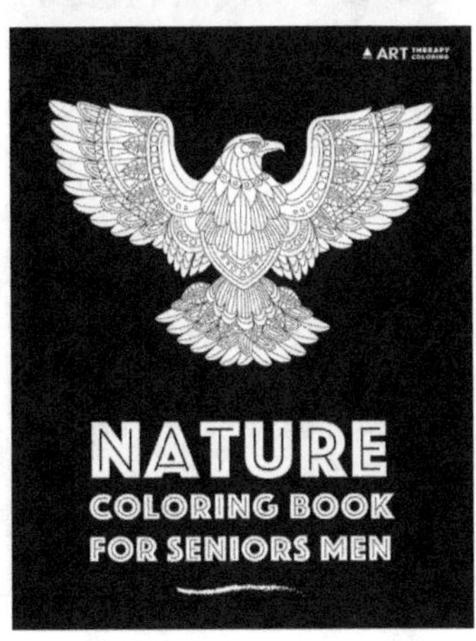
NATURE
COLORING BOOK
FOR SENIORS MEN

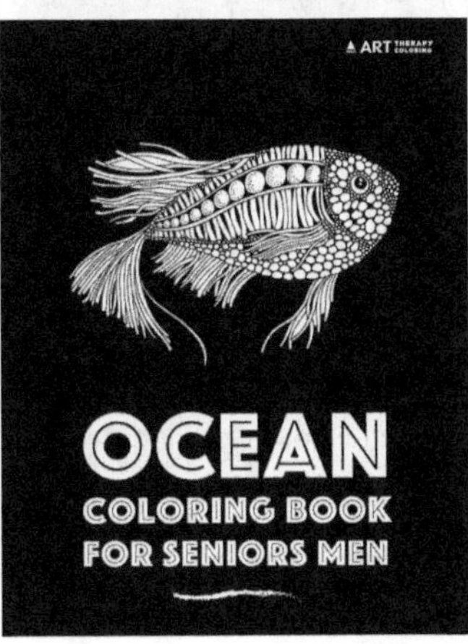
OCEAN
COLORING BOOK
FOR SENIORS MEN

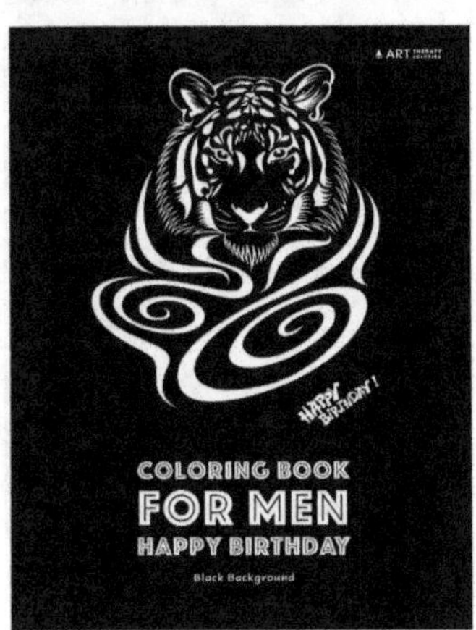
HAPPY BIRTHDAY!
COLORING BOOK
FOR MEN
HAPPY BIRTHDAY
Black Background

Coloring Books For Special Occasions

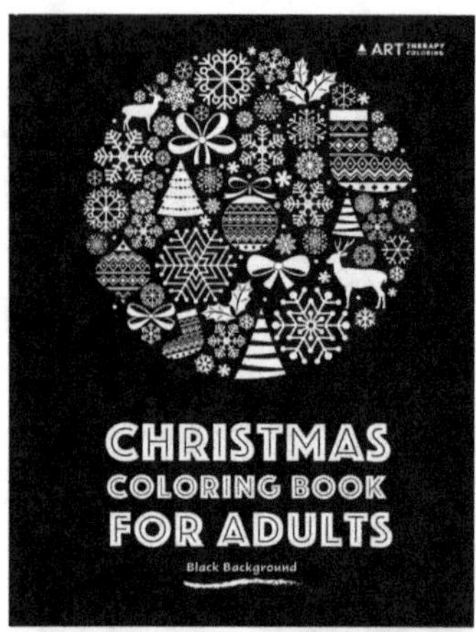
ART THERAPY COLORING
CHRISTMAS
COLORING BOOK
FOR ADULTS
Black Background

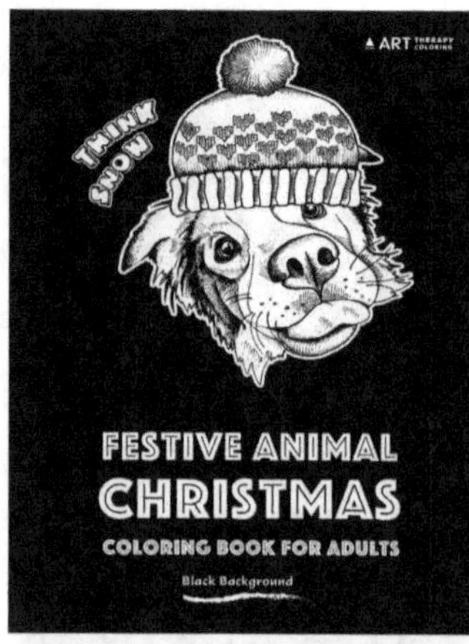
ART THERAPY COLORING
FESTIVE ANIMAL
CHRISTMAS
COLORING BOOK FOR ADULTS
Black Background

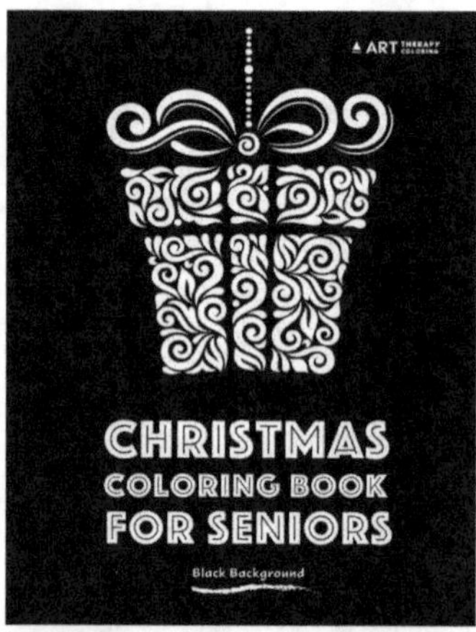
ART THERAPY COLORING
CHRISTMAS
COLORING BOOK
FOR SENIORS
Black Background

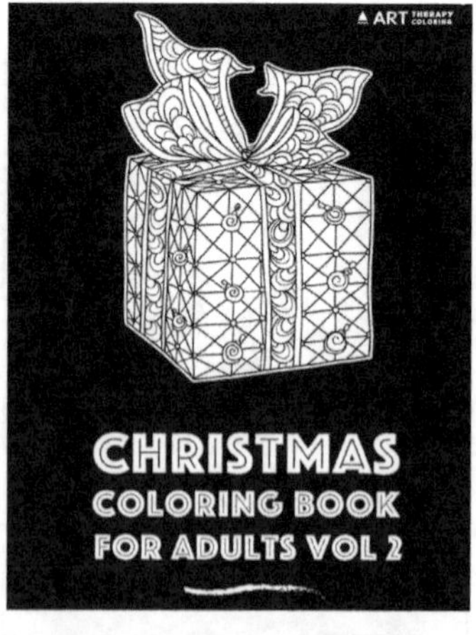
ART THERAPY COLORING
CHRISTMAS
COLORING BOOK
FOR ADULTS VOL 2

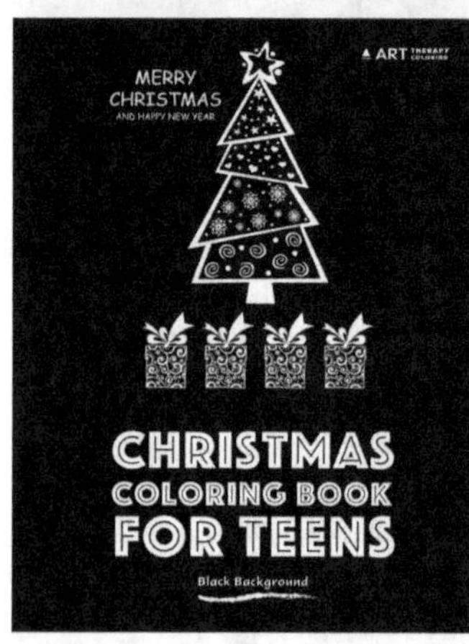
ART THERAPY COLORING
MERRY
CHRISTMAS
CHRISTMAS
COLORING BOOK
FOR TEENS
Black Background

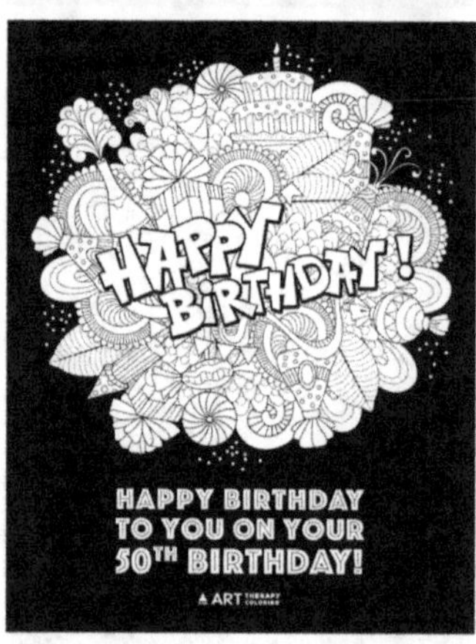
HAPPY BIRTHDAY!
HAPPY BIRTHDAY
TO YOU ON YOUR
50TH BIRTHDAY!
ART THERAPY COLORING

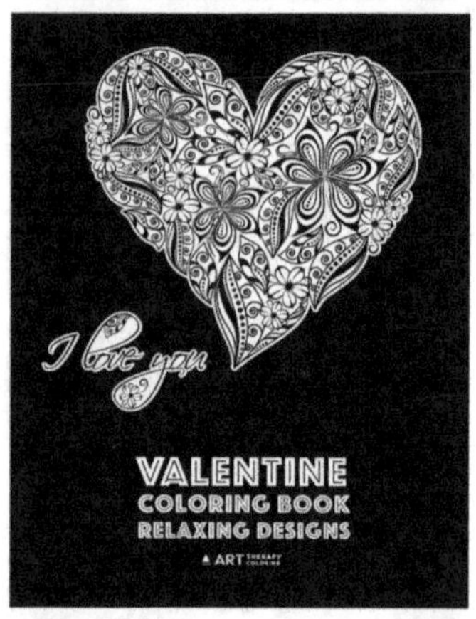
I love you
VALENTINE
COLORING BOOK
RELAXING DESIGNS
ART THERAPY COLORING

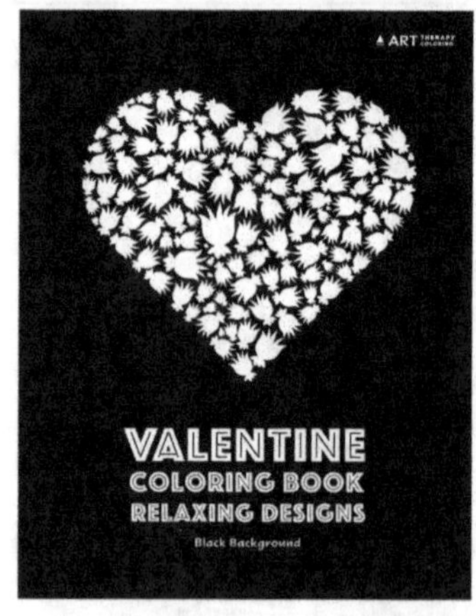
ART THERAPY COLORING
VALENTINE
COLORING BOOK
RELAXING DESIGNS
Black Background

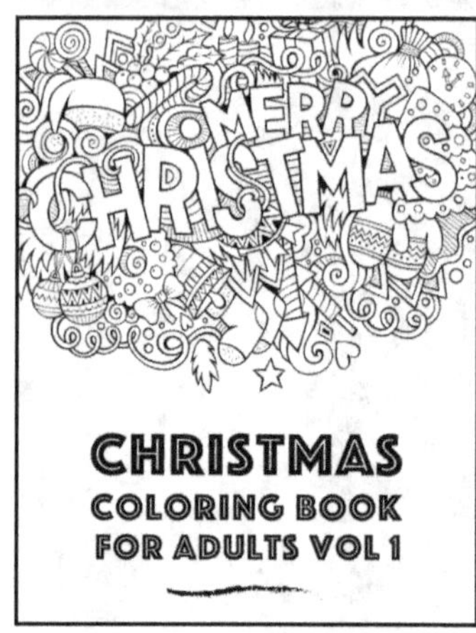
MERRY
CHRISTMAS
CHRISTMAS
COLORING BOOK
FOR ADULTS VOL 1

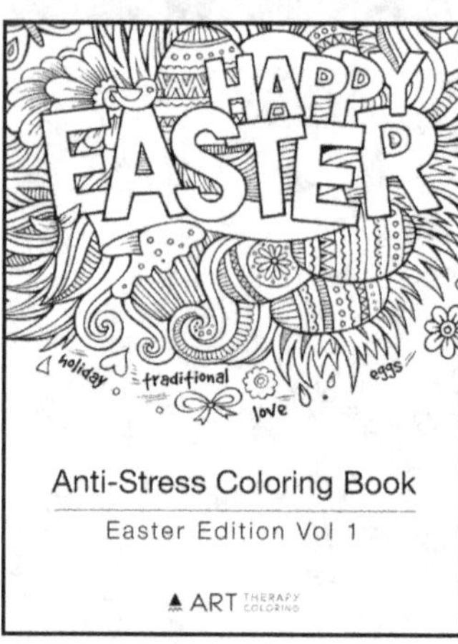
HAPPY
EASTER
holiday
traditional
love
eggs
Anti-Stress Coloring Book
Easter Edition Vol 1
ART THERAPY COLORING

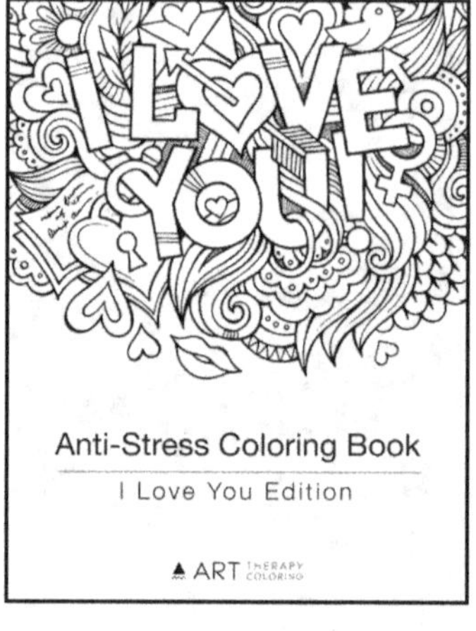
I LOVE YOU!
Anti-Stress Coloring Book
I Love You Edition
ART THERAPY COLORING

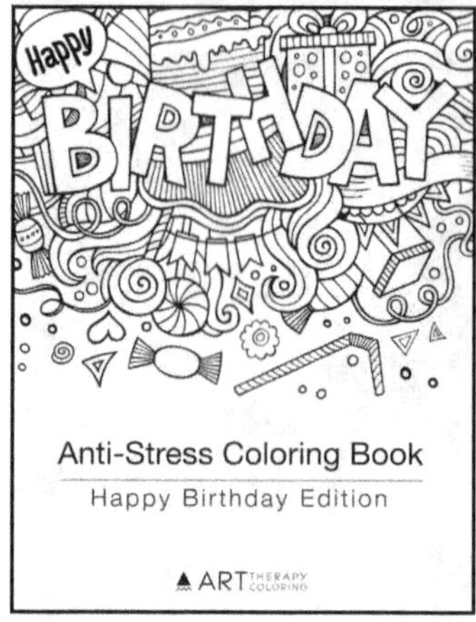
Happy
BIRTHDAY
Anti-Stress Coloring Book
Happy Birthday Edition
ART THERAPY COLORING

Coloring Book For Teens
Anti-Stress Designs Vol 3

Published by:
Art Therapy Coloring
El Dorado Hills, California
www.arttherapycoloring.com

Shutterstock Images

ISBN: 978-1-944427-18-4

www.ingramcontent.com/pod-product-compliance
Lightning Source LLC
LaVergne TN
LVHW080335110826
845155LV00027B/247

* 9 7 8 1 9 4 4 4 2 7 1 8 4 *